From Sea to Shining Sea

PLACES THAT SHAPED AMERICA

Lenn Schramm
Photography by Elan Penn

Foreword by Senator George Mitchell

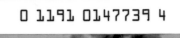

STERLING PUBLISHING CO., INC., NEW YORK

Edited and arranged by Jeanette Green
Designed by Richard Oriolo
Cartography by Michel Opatowski

LIBRARY OF CONGRESS CATALOGING-IN-PUBLICATION DATA

Schramm, Lenn.
    From sea to shining sea : places that shaped America / Lenn Schramm ;
photography by Elan Penn ; foreword by Senator George Mitchell.
        p. cm.
    Includes index.
    ISBN 1-4027-0414-3
  1. Historic sites—United States. 2. Historic sites—United States—Pictorial works. 3. United States—History, Local.
  4. United States—History, Local—Pictorial works. 5. United States—Description and travel. I. Title.
E159.S37 2003
973'.022'2—dc21   2003000290

2 4 6 8 10 9 7 5 3 1

Published by Sterling Publishing Co., Inc.
387 Park Avenue South, New York, NY 10016
© 2003 by Penn Publishing, Ltd.
Distributed in Canada by Sterling Publishing
C/o Canadian Manda Group, One Atlantic Avenue, Suite 105
Toronto, Ontario, Canada M6K 3E7
Distributed in Great Britain by Chrysalis Books
64 Brewery Road, London N7 9NT, England
Distributed in Australia by Capricorn Link (Australia) Pty. Ltd.
P.O. Box 704, Windsor, NSW 2756 Australia
Printed in China
All rights reserved

Sterling ISBN 1-4027-0414-3

ACKNOWLEDGMENTS
We acknowledge the assistance of the Mount Vernon Ladies' Association, which owns and operates Mount Vernon; the Hawaii Visitors' & Convention Bureau; Ulster County Tourism, New York; the Thomas Jefferson Foundation, Inc.; the U.S.S. *Missouri* Memorial Association; the Mark Twain Museum, Hannibal, Missouri; the Hancock Shaker Village, Pittsfield, Massachusetts; the Texas Cowboy Hall of Fame, Fort Worth, Texas; Oak Alley Plantation, Vacherie, Louisiana; Erie Canal Village, Rome, New York; Plimoth Plantation, Plymouth, Massachusetts; Henry Ford Museum & Greenfield Village, Dearborn, Michigan; Maine photographer Kevin Byron; and helpful park rangers across America.

    We warmly thank the Honorable Senator George Mitchell for taking time out of his busy schedule to write the Foreword; we are honored to print his words here. We also thank Brenda Chapman-Barnes, assistant to Senator Mitchell at Piper Rudnick, LLP, for her gracious assistance. Colleagues, authors, and friends across the United States offered fresh perspectives, subject or technical expertise, and suggested places important in shaping the America we know today. We especially thank Rick Willett, Claire Bazinet, Karen Backstein, Makéda Abdullah, Irene Lee, Rodman Neumann, Michael Beacom, Isabel Stein, John Woodside, Jeannine Ford, Eileen Laibinis, and Emma Gonzalez at Sterling. We also thank Clare Palmieri, Tamías ben-Magid, Kathryn Augustin, Laura Halford Sparrow, Dana Muller, Jack Deeney, Danielle Moretti-Langholtz, Richard Green, and David Jones for their sure wisdom and fact-checking.

PHOTOS
TITLE PAGE: The Jefferson Memorial, Tidal Basin, Washington, D.C. COVER: *(top)* Dalton Highway and Brooks Range, Alaska pipeline, Alaska. © Corbis. *(bottom)* Capitol Building, Washington, D.C.

Site selection by Steve Magnuson and Jeanette Green
Certain site histories, passages, and boxes by the editor

Dedicated to the People of America

HISTORIC SITES

LOCATING THE PLACES ON THE AMERICAN MAP

These are the places that have shaped America. Although you know our country firsthand, we thought you'd like to locate them yourself on a map. And you may want to visit them. Of course every city, town, village, farmer's field, road, mountain, river, lake, pond, stream, stump, flower, and tree has contributed to making our great nation. But most important, all of you have shaped America. Without the many voices of its citizens, our democracy would fail. America from the very beginning has been the heart and mind of its people. This living experiment, this democracy, depends on all of us.

Contents

Portland Head Light, Cape Elizabeth, Maine. © *Kevin Byron.*

Foreword

by Senator George Mitchell

Every society in human history has been shaped by geography. The United States is no exception. Blessed with a large, resource-filled continent, protected by the world's two largest oceans, early Americans developed the optimism and faith in the future that has come to characterize our society.

As we enter the third century of our national existence, that optimism and faith have been vindicated. The U.S. is the world's dominant economic and military power.

That role brings with it enormous benefits and many problems. In this era of instant communication, every problem in the world is seen by some as an American problem. Every grievance, no matter how local, whether real or imagined, can be a cause for resentment of the dominant power.

In the past few years, I've met with political and business leaders from many countries in Europe, from Ireland to Russia, from Scandinavia to the Mediterranean Sea. I asked them this question: Now that the Soviet Union no longer exists and Russia has withdrawn its military forces back to its own territory, do you think the U.S. should withdraw our forces back to our own territory?

Without exception the answer was an emphatic no. Think back through history and try to recall a dominant power with so much moral authority that many other countries asked that its military forces be stationed on their soil.

Why is that? Obviously, part of it lies in the power itself. But I am concerned that, for many Americans, power is perceived to be the exclusive basis of American influence in the world.

Surely, there's more than power involved. I believe that the primary basis of American influence in the world always has been our basic ideals: individual liberty, equal justice, and opportunity for all.

We must never forget that the United States was a great nation long before it was a great economic or military power. When there were fewer than four million Americans clinging to the Atlantic seaboard, this was a great nation, ennobled by the Declaration of Independence and the American Constitution.

These charter documents, especially the Bill of Rights, the first ten amendments to the Constitution, are the most eloquent and concise statements of individual liberty ever written and adopted by human beings.

Yet, great as the founding fathers were, they were products of their time, constrained by the society in which they learned and lived.

So the Constitution, which we rightly revere, limited the right to vote to adult white men who owned property. Black persons were not even considered to be persons. It took seventy-five years and the bloodiest war in our history to extend the right to vote to all adult males.

It took another sixty years, and a bitter political struggle, to extend it to women.

And it was just a decade ago that Americans with disabilities were given the legal right to live full and meaningful lives.

To this day the struggle goes on, to expand our definition of citizenship, of the human and civil rights which each American should enjoy.

It is both a painful record and inspiring evidence of what is great about America, a never-ending effort to right the wrongs of the past, to enable each generation to be more free and more prosperous than its predecessor.

We have just entered what will be the first full century of American dominance in the world. It can be, like so many in the past, a century of war and famine, of oppression and injustice. But it also can be a time when the dominant power uses its strength carefully and with purpose, and commits its people, its power, and its prestige to a noble vision: a world that is largely at peace, with education, opportunity, and prosperity extending to more and more people in more and more parts of the world.

That is our challenge. We must make it our destiny.

In colorful photographs and powerful, contemporaneous words, *From Sea to Shining Sea* identifies and illuminates the places that shaped and recorded America's destiny. They include many sites and cover three centuries: from the first colony at Jamestown to the first capital city at Santa Fe; from the seaports of New England to the cotton fields of the South to the wilderness of Alaska; from Valley Forge to Gettysburg to Ground Zero; it's all here, in a format that will both inform and delight the reader.

We Americans are the most fortunate people ever to have lived, citizens of the most free, the most open, the most just society in history. Most of us are Americans by accident of birth. But America was built by immigrants who became citizens by choice. Some came to escape religious persecution or political oppression, some to join families already here. Most came to seek a better life in a land of freedom and opportunity. America is so big, so diverse, so full of energy that it cannot fairly be summed up in a few words. But I'd like to try by telling a personal story.

Before I entered the Senate, I had the privilege of serving as a federal district court judge. Occasionally, I presided over naturalization ceremonies, where immigrants are sworn in as citizens. I've never done anything more meaningful or enjoyable.

In these ceremonies the new citizens-to-be gathered before me in a federal courtroom. They had come from every part of the world and had gone through the required procedures. Then I administered to them the oath of allegiance to the United States and made them Americans.

The Honorable Senator George Mitchell

It was always an emotional moment for me. My mother was an immigrant; my father the orphan son of immigrants. They had no education. My mother could not read or write English, and for her entire adult life she worked the night shift in a textile mill. My father was a janitor. But because of their efforts and, more importantly, because of the openness of American society, I, their son, was able to become the Majority Leader of the United States Senate. I believe in the American dream because I have lived it.

After every ceremony I spoke with each of the new citizens. Their devotion to, and enthusiasm for, the country of their choice was inspiring. I asked them why they came, how they came, what they hoped to find here. Their answers were as different as their countries of origin. But through them all ran a common theme, best expressed by a young man from Asia who, when I asked why he came, answered slowly, in halting English, "I came because here in America everybody has a chance." That young man, who had been an American for only a few minutes, summed up the meaning of our country in one sentence. America is freedom and opportunity.

From Sea to Shining Sea helps us understand where and how it happened.

Introduction

New Yorkers often joke that their bustling metropolis "will be a great place—when they finish it." The roar of jackhammers, the aroma of fresh asphalt, and miles of scaffolding remind residents and visitors alike that the nation's largest city is a virtual crazy quilt of constant construction.

The United States is likewise a work-in-progress, its 9.6 million square miles a sprawling, ever-changing tapestry woven from threads ancient and modern, native and foreign, natural and man-made.

Stretched across eight time zones, the sheer geographic sweep of the United States and its territories has ensured that change and diversity are central themes in American life. Without leaving U.S. soil, a traveler can tackle a 20,000-foot-high mountain peak (Denali in Alaska), cross a parched desert more than 200 feet below sea level (Death Valley in California), navigate rivers for thousands of miles to the Atlantic, Pacific, and Gulf of Mexico, and experience weather ranging from tropical highs to bone-chilling arctic lows. A driver on the nation's intricate web of roadways sees pastoral countryside change into small towns, suburbs, and cities, and back again. Transcontinental pilots and passengers glide above a monumental ocean-to-ocean patchwork quilt of fields, forests, lakes, and mountains.

Diversity is not limited to the country's geography. The nation's vast spaces and varied terrain are also home to over 280 million people from every walk of life. From Native Americans boasting centuries-old roots on the continent to new and not-so-new immigrants, the world's self-proclaimed "melting pot" has absorbed and assimilated generations of individuals representing every ethnic group, religious belief, political persuasion, and economic class.

Given the multifaceted nature of the United States, the task of identifying fewer than a hundred places that have "shaped" its identity is a daunting one. Thousands of historic sites dot the national landscape. The National Park Service alone runs more than four hundred. Other federal agencies and state and local governments act as custodians for thousands more. Still others are in the hands of local historical societies, volunteer groups, and private owners. Each one has a tale, large or small, to contribute to the national story.

To make matters even more interesting, some historically significant places are not pinpoint historic "sites" in the traditional sense. Hollywood is a good example. The movie studios and film industry of Tinseltown are intimately tied up with our national identity, yet it would be difficult to select any single spot in Hollywood that has shaped the country. Another example is the Underground Railroad of the mid-19th century. No one "station" on the escape route North was more important than another; together they all served a vital purpose in the eyes of Southern slaves and their benefactors.

Even well-known historic sites aren't always as straightforward as they appear. One site can mean different things to different people. Around the turn of the century, the nation's two main immigration entry points—Ellis Island on the East Coast and Angel Island on the West Coast—represented doors to opportunity or frustrating barriers, depending upon a person's experience there. The Lincoln Memorial is both a serene and majestic tribute to our 16th president as well as the site of two of the most dramatic moments in the country's Civil Rights Movement: African-American diva Marian Anderson's concert in April 1939 and the Rev. Dr. Martin Luther King, Jr.'s "I Have a Dream" speech in 1963. Well before its unveiling in 1982, the Vietnam Veterans Memorial in Washington, D.C., provoked fierce debate, protests, cheers, disappointment, pride, and tears—much like the Vietnam War itself. Many other historic sites likewise offer meanings as complex, conflicted—and diverse—as the nation itself.

Given the mind-boggling array of choices and multiple meanings of many historic landmarks, how were the "places that shaped America" selected? With a list of possibilities in hand (that we kept to ourselves), we surveyed colleagues, authors, and friends across the country to gain a voice or consensus of honored places and to hear fresh ideas. Then we culled the list with an eye to representing the many facets of the American personality. Our aim was to celebrate the American people rather than individual heroes and to describe our social history as a democracy rather than to review political programs or presidential careers. The majority of places chosen for this book fall into the category of classics—patriotic historic sites with which most Americans are familiar. But included, too, are a few places sure to surprise. All have a kind of symbolic significance meant to suggest events, industries, movements, spirits, impulses, and moods larger than themselves.

We wanted to focus on places that evoke a sort of national memory independent of pop culture or high art. Instead of Disneyland, we chose Hollywood and Broadway; rather than McDonald's, we favored American farms and stockyards; and rather than sports arenas, we include the meeting places of democratic ideas, social reforms, and living experiments—churches, the African Meeting House, Hancock Shaker Village, the Old State House, the Capitol, the Lincoln Memorial, and more.

Among the sites chosen are places that many Americans hold nearly sacred: Mount Rushmore in South Dakota; Jamestown, Williamsburg, and Thomas Jefferson's beloved "little mountain" retreat, Monticello, in Virginia; Independence Hall, the Liberty Bell, the Betsy Ross House, and Valley Forge in or near Philadelphia; the Old North Church and Bunker Hill in Boston; the Jefferson, Lincoln, and Washington memorials in Washington, D.C., together with the White House, U.S. Capitol, and the U.S. Supreme Court.

Other places reflect Americans' perennial fascination with the origins of ideas and things. New Orleans, for example, gave birth to jazz in the late 1800s, while Nashville's Grand Ole Opry has midwived and nurtured many of the nation's biggest country music stars since 1925. Thomas Edison's laboratory at Menlo Park, New Jersey; Los Alamos National Laboratory; and the "garage" incubators of California's Silicon Valley have been birthplaces of key developments in U.S. science and engineering.

Any book professing to highlight places that have shaped the country's identity must include historic sites from the annals of the country's free-enterprise system. Nantucket, Massachusetts, brings to mind the great whaling and seafaring industries of the Eastern seaboard dating from the 17th century. West Virginia is synonymous with coal mines, while the South's identity is intimately bound up with cotton. The stockyards of Chicago and Fort Worth conjure up images of cowboys, cattle drives, and the Old West. And Detroit, established in 1701 as a humble French fur-trading post, grew into a 20th century industrial giant. Its growth was inspired by an inventive spirit, born and bred in the United States, which has turned the nation's economy into a global power.

The country's "can-do" attitude is captured in other ways as well. The early skyscrapers of Chicago and New York, as well as Hoover Dam, symbolize the triumph of human ingenuity over the forces of nature. In Promontory, Utah, and Council Bluffs, Iowa, golden spikes celebrate the country's determination to unite with rails its far-flung regions in the mid-19th century. Places like Kill Devil Hills, near Kitty Hawk, and Cape Canaveral capture a century of American ambition to conquer air and space, the last great frontier.

Freedom of expression is another defining element of the country's character, including the right of groups to gather and express themselves freely on any subject. Nineteenth century audiences at the African Meeting House in Boston, for example, heard prominent abolitionists hold forth on the evils of slavery; such meetings pushed the country along the path toward both civil war and civil rights. The Hancock Shaker Village exemplifies places where people of strong beliefs have come together to worship or live together in peace. Since its construction in 1695, the Wren Building on William and Mary's campus in Williamsburg, Virginia, has seen the uncensored discussion of ideas by professors and students (among them, Thomas Jefferson) for more than three centuries. Other meeting places are truly national in nature, such as the stretch of the Mall in front of the Lincoln Memorial and the Washington Monument in Washington, D.C.

Of course, not every well-known gathering place has brought together Americans of like mind. Many historic sites proudly commemorate important moments of confrontation and contest: events or people who have challenged the status quo, stood up for their rights, and tested our ideals as a nation. Military sites like Fort McHenry, Fort Ticonderoga, Gettysburg, Fort Sumter, Vicksburg, and Appomattox all remind us of battles lost and won in the name of a cause. The women's rights convention at Seneca Falls in 1848 kicked off a campaign for equality that continues today. The road from Selma to Montgomery, Alabama, and other key Civil Rights sites throughout the South likewise memorialize the country's struggle to live up to its commitment to treat all its citizens with dignity, an ideal also symbolized by the imposing facade of the U.S. Supreme Court in Washington, D.C.

Other important events that have left a stamp on the nation's psyche touch on dark hours or tragedies that have taught lessons or united the country. The site of the Salem witch trials of 1692, for example, reminds us even today of the dangers of intolerance. The 1911 Triangle Shirtwaist Factory fire, in which 146 women and children died on the job, helped to galvanize the country to protect the health and safety of its labor force. The attacks on Pearl Harbor in 1941, and on the World Trade Center and the Pentagon sixty years later, drew the nation together as few other events have ever done.

Some sites that have played major roles in shaping the country are literally part of the national landscape. The Great Lakes, mountains, rivers, deserts, and vast stretches of plains have all had an impact on the nation's development, in some cases by providing an obstacle to be surmounted, and in others, by supplying an important transportation route. An intrepid traveler who traces the Lewis & Clark Trail, Santa Fe Trail, Hudson River, and the Erie Canal, for example, can appreciate first-hand the impact of geography on the human determination to move, explore, and connect. Other features in the landscape have been taken into the nation's heart because their rugged splendor reflects an equally rugged American spirit. The colors of Canyon de Chelly, the majesty of Yellowstone, and the exotic wilds of Alaska rival any landscape in the world for beauty and bounty.

And, finally, a few notable places are less about location than about the American imagination. Legendary Route 66, for example, is not merely a line on a map, but the embodiment of the quintessentially American urge to be on the move. Dodge City, the beginning of law and order in the West, is an emotional touchstone for those drawn to a romantic view of the American frontier. Greenwich Village and Wall Street—sitting cheek-by-jowl on the southern tip of Manhattan—are light-years apart in terms of the lifestyles and ambitions each symbolize. Farther south, magnolia-studded plantations and the muddy Mississippi call up competing images of injustice and idyllic living. And the tiny one-room schoolhouses that dot the countryside from coast-to-coast are far more than four simple walls; they are powerful and nostalgic icons of an earlier era in the American past. They represent the importance of universal education to the development of a shining democracy.

In her 1993 memoir, *Dakota*, poet Kathleen Norris meditates on the subtle but seminal role that location plays in forming its human inhabitants. Her thoughts are focused on South Dakota, but Norris could easily be speaking of the entire American landscape:

"The sense of place is unavoidable in western Dakota, and maybe that's our gift to the world...In these places you wait, and the places mold you."

—KATHI ANN BROWN

CANYON DE CHELLY
First Peoples of the Americas

CHINLE, ARIZONA

The notion that Columbus or Leif Eriksson "discovered" America is of course nonsense. The aborigines, or first peoples, whom the newly arrived Europeans called Indians, had been living in North America for millennia.

Because of the United States' predominantly moist climate and the fact that most natives relied on wood and other perishable materials for buildings and artifacts, we have few salient reminders of the ancient prehistory of these first peoples. In the Southwest, however, an Egyptlike aridity has preserved the remains of a

Junction Overlook, South Rim Drive, Canyon de Chelly National Monument, Arizona.

remarkable culture more than 2,000 years old. Canyon de Chelly in northeastern Arizona, Carl Jung remarked, embodies the essence of antiquity more than any place outside the Nile Valley.

The name *Chelly* derives from a Navajo word, *tségi*, or "rock canyon." Spanish and Mexican soldiers and explorers hispanized this to *chelli* or something similar. Subsequently anglicized, today the name is generally pronounced *de-shay*.

Available water and practical defensibility made Canyon de Chelly a center of human habitation some 5,000 years ago. Most of the more than 800 known archaeological sites within the 131-square-mile Canyon de Chelly date to the period A.D. 350–1300, however. They include pit-houses and the later (after A.D. 700) masonry cliff dwellings or *pueblos*, built high on the canyon walls out of reach of enemies and floods. These cliff houses are associated with the Anasazi (Navajo for "enemy forebears"), ancestors of modern-day Pueblo Indians, whose culture flowered in the 12th and 13th centuries.

Spider Rock at sunset, Canyon de Chelly National Monument, Arizona.

The Anasazi occupied the Four Corners region of the southern Colorado Plateau and upper Rio Grande—present-day northeastern Arizona, northwestern New Mexico, southeastern Utah, and southwestern Colorado. They left spectacular ruins throughout this area, notably at Mesa Verde in Colorado.

At first these people did not make pottery; instead, they excelled at basketry and are commonly referred to today as the Basket Makers. In addition to hunting, initially with spears sent flying with the aid of the throwing device we call the *atlatl*, and later with bow and arrow, they raised maize and squash. Later they added beans to their dietary repertoire and domesticated the dog and turkey.

Sometime around the year 1300, in part because of climatic changes that reduced agricultural yields, but also, scientists now believe, due to social and perhaps religious upheaval, the Anasazi culture abandoned its villages in the Four Corners region and vanished from the historical stage.

In later centuries, early Hopis occupied Canyon de Chelly sporadically, whenever there was enough water to raise crops. The Navajos invaded about 300 years later, at the end of the long dry period. They managed to subdue other tribes of the region but were overmatched when they took on the Spaniards of Mexico and, after 1848, the United States.

In addition to the spectacular scenery and remains of habitations, Canyon de Chelly is noteworthy for its petroglyphs and pictographs. These rock art representations are the only historical records that the Native Americans, without the benefit of a written language, left behind.

"The Navajo have a story about how the Canyon de Chelly was made....One day Coyote went to the People and begged them to show him how to use fire. The People gave him their flint stones. Coyote tried and tried to make fire with them, but with no luck. In anger he flung the stones to the ground, which started a fire so big and hot that the earth split. Then Water Pourer poured water into the crack, and the washing action of the water gradually enlarged it."

—Alex Shoumatoff, *Legends of the American Desert* (1997)

AMERICAN INDIAN VILLAGES
Before the Europeans Came

"These native villages are as unchanging as the woman in one of their stories. When she was called before a local justice, he asked her age. 'I have 45 years.' 'But,' said the justice, 'you were 45 when you appeared before me two years ago.' 'Señor Judge,' she replied proudly, drawing herself to her full height, 'I am not of those who are one thing today and another tomorrow.'"—New Mexico: A Guide to the Colorful State (1940)

LANDS FROM THE ATLANTIC TO THE PACIFIC OCEAN, AND ISLANDS BEYOND

If all aboriginal inhabitants of the future United States had vanished before the first Europeans landed, hundreds of mounds in the Mississippi and Ohio valleys and the pueblos of the Southwest would be the only obvious sign of their presence. Aside from these mounds and pueblos, they built no enduring monuments or public works. Outside the arid Southwest, their typical forms of shelter were transient: the wigwam and longhouse of the eastern woodland tribes; the earth-covered hogan of the Navajo and earth-covered lodge of the north-central plains; the thatched plaster-walled house of the southeast; the Seminole chickee or stilt house; the wickiup of the Great Basin and California; the plank house and forest longhouse of the Pacific Northwest; and the buffalo-hide tepee of the Great Plains.

European colonists arriving in the 16th century marveled at the new American Eden, with its unspoiled lands. We have to thank American Indians for their respect and reverence for the land.

In the creation story of the Diné (Navajo) people, the first hogan was the gods' gift to humankind. The original design had a wooden frame and five sides of packed earth, sometimes covered with adobe or mud for insulation. In the early 20th century, the availability of railroad crossties inspired much roomier wood-sided hexagonal or octagonal hogans.

Around A.D. 700, the tribes of the Southwest began building cliffside homes of sandstone and mud mortar, chinked with small stones and covered with a thin coat of plaster. A similar design, but with adobe substituting for the unavailable sandstone, was used in desert flatlands. Over the centuries, these grew from single-family residences to large, interconnected, multifamily dwellings. This is what the Spanish saw when they first penetrated the area; they called the complexes *pueblos,* "towns" or "villages" in Spanish. Mesa Verde in Colorado, with more than 200 rooms, is one of the most spectacular sites of the earlier pueblo period, before the year 1300. Pueblo Bonito, in New Mexico, had more than 800 rooms in its prime. Even after these and similar sites were abandoned, the pueblo design remained in vogue. There are several more recent and never-abandoned pueblo communities, including Acoma and Taos, in New Mexico. The latter, which dates from the 15th century, was an important center of resistance to the Spanish in the 17th and 18th centuries.

The woodland nations of the northeast lived in small, dome-shaped, one-family birch-bark wigwams, built from scratch each season. A frame of poles was covered with mats of woven reeds and then with dirt and sod, or bark and animal skins, depending on the season and climate. Later, the Iroquois nations preferred longhouses of similar construction, which sheltered multiple families and were frequently preserved from year to year.

Taos Pueblo, New Mexico. The multistoried adobe buildings have been continuously inhabited for over 1,000 years.

Cliff Palace, Mesa Verde National Park, Colorado. The culture represented at Mesa Verde reflects more than 700 years of history. From about A.D. 600 to 1300 people lived and flourished in communities throughout the area, eventually building elaborate stone villages in the sheltered alcoves of the canyon walls, "cliff dwellings." The cliff dwellings represent the last 75 to 100 years of occupation at Mesa Verde. In the late 1200s, within the span of one or two generations, they left their homes and moved away.

The sedentary tribes of the northern plains favored wood-frame structures with slanted walls, covered with willow, brush, and a thick layer of dirt. These, too, were meant to last for a number of years.

The small, cone-shaped bark tepee, based on the eastern wigwam, was used by the largely agricultural people of the Great Plains. But the introduction of the horse in the 17th century radically transformed their lifestyle. Hunting bison from horseback was safe and efficient; the beasts were so plentiful that starvation was no longer a threat. The tribes abandoned their sedentary existence and developed a nomadic culture that followed the bison. Their new lifestyle required a portable dwelling. Sometime in the 18th century the small tepee was adapted into a larger version, covered with 15 to 50 bison hides. This tepee was warm in winter and cool in summer, waterproof, and resistant to winter gales. It could be erected and struck quickly and was readily transportable on a travois made of its own poles.

It seems fitting that, for modern Americans, it is the tepee—the most temporary structure of all, both in its mode of use and the brevity of its dominance—that has become the paradigmatic dwelling of the American Indian.

SANTA FE

America's Oldest Capital City: Spanish, Indian & Mexican Rule

"Santa Fe was not merely my state of mind. It was really an interesting place—possibly the only town of its kind anywhere." —Emily Hahn's memoir, describing Santa Fe in 1927

SANTA FE, NEW MEXICO

For centuries, what is now New Mexico was home to tribes of the Pueblo culture. In the 15th century, Athapascan peoples—the Apache and Navajo—invaded from the north. Shortly thereafter, the Spanish arrived from the south, bringing Catholic priests, horses, long-horned cattle, advanced technology (including the wheel), European food crops, and disease germs.

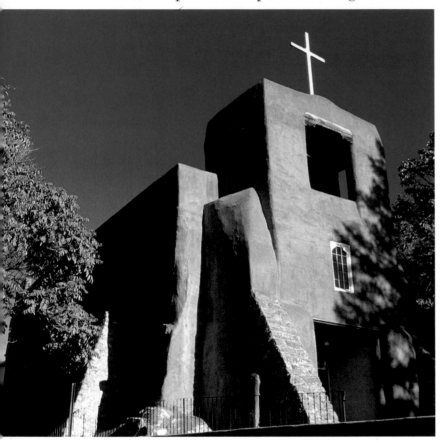

San Miguel Church, Santa Fe, New Mexico. San Miguel is the oldest church structure in the United States. In about 1610, Tlaxcalan Indians from Mexico built the original adobe walls and altar under the direction of Franciscan padres.

In the 1848 treaty of Guadalupe-Hidalgo, the United States acquired the territory of New Mexico. At this time, the territory had 70,000 Spanish settlers and only a few U.S. settlers. In 1912 New Mexico became the 47th state.

The Spanish occupation of the American mainland began with Hernando Cortés's conquest of the Aztec empire in Mexico (1519–1521). During the next several decades, a succession of adventurer-explorers—Hernando de Soto, Francisco Vásquez de Coronado, and others—penetrated what are now the Gulf States, the lower Mississippi Valley, and the lands stretching from New Mexico to Kansas, looking for fabled cities whose wealth, like that of Mexico, could be carted away. Not finding them, the Spanish turned their attention to South America. Northward expansion into Nuevo México had low priority.

The 16th century was almost over before the slow tide of colonization reached the Río Grande. In 1598, Juan de Oñate established an outpost at the confluence of the Río Chama and Río Grande to serve as the capital of Nuevo México. At the end of the next decade it was replaced by newly founded Santa Fe, built in 1607–1610 on the site of an abandoned pueblo. The Palace of the Governors, the oldest seat of civil government in the United States, was one of Santa Fe's first buildings (built in 1610). Over the next seven decades, a thin stream of colonists made the long six-month trek north from Mexico (in 1680 there were fewer than 4,000 Europeans in Nuevo México).

Spanish rulers, colonists, and priests exploited and abused American Indians, whose resentment exploded in 1680. Led by the chief of the Taos pueblo, the natives staged a carefully planned and coordinated uprising. They invaded and plundered farms, ranches, and missions across New Mexico; procured horses and guns; and drove the Spanish soldiers and settlers all the way back to El Paso. They sacked Santa Fe; the Palace of the Governors survived the destruction. The Pueblo Revolt was the greatest setback for European expansion in North America that native Indian populations ever inflicted.

Twelve years later, the Spanish returned cautiously, keeping both cross and sword under wraps. Meanwhile, Navajos and Apaches had been raiding the Pueblos relentlessly, leading many pueblo-dwellers to decide they preferred the security offered by Spanish overlordship. The new Spanish governor, Don Diego de Vargas, reclaimed Santa Fe without violence. Franciscans also softened their approach and accepted a measure of syncretism of Native American rituals and celebrations with Catholic ones.

For the Spanish, acculturation of the natives was the only way to secure their North American dominions against the French and the English, who had been much more successful in attracting their own citizens to the New World. While the French and English colonies consisted of freeholders, Spain transplanted its rigidly hierarchical society to the New World. European-born *peninsulares* lorded it over those born in Mexico (*criollos*). In the absence of a self-sustaining community of immigrants, Spanish and Mexican men were much more likely to marry native women than were men in New England and Virginia. This created a

Fort Union National Monument, New Mexico, is located 75 miles from Santa Fe. The fort was part of the defense of the Santa Fe Trail. The trail began on the west bank of the Missouri River, led west to Fort Dodge, Kansas, and forked. One route ran southwest and one west; both trails merged just beyond Fort Union.

caste of *mestizos*, with both Spanish and Indian heritage, who, along with Christianized Indians or *genízaros*, formed most of the so-called Hispanic population of Mexico and Nuevo México. Until 1775, the residents of the thirteen colonies considered themselves to be Englishmen and Englishwomen, equal to all of King George's other loyal subjects. *Criollos* and *mestizos* were allowed no parallel delusion.

In contrast with New Mexico (Nuevo México), the United States was founded in part by people who sought religious freedom as well as the privilege of self-government and democratic rights. Santa Fe's Palace of Governors long antedates Boston's Old State House and Philadelphia's Independence Hall. However, although four flags—Spanish, American Indian, Mexican, and American—have flown over the palace, only under the Stars and Stripes did it serve as a seat of representative government.

Only about 5,000 Mexicans lived in Texas in 1835, compared to 20,000 Anglos. In 1848, less than 6,000 non-Indian civilians lived in California. Only New Mexico, with a population of about 60,000 in 1848, had a consolidated Spanish society before coming under U.S. control. In the succeeding centuries, millions of people, seeking greater opportunity and freedom, have migrated from Latin America and settled in the American Southwest and in the cities, towns, and farms of California.

SPANISH MISSIONS
Catholic Priests & Reluctant Indian Converts

NEW MEXICO, ARIZONA, TEXAS, AND CALIFORNIA

In the 17th century, as Spain began to establish colonies in Mexico and what is today the American Southwest (and later in California), Franciscan priests, fired by their religious zeal to convert the heathen Indians, soon followed conquistadors, adventurers, and colonists. In spreading Christianity they expedited the spread of Spanish culture and Spanish rule, so Franciscan missionaries enjoyed royal support for their New World endeavors. More than 70 pueblo villages were renamed for a saint and their residents forced into the rigid mold of Spanish Catholicism.

Spanish missions taught new agriculture techniques and crafts and later provided schooling to American Indian populations. They offered medical care as European diseases ravaged native villages.

Spain, of course, was then the home of the Inquisition. Although the Inquisition was begun under the rigorous Catholicism of 13th century France, and not championed by Franciscans, Indian natives whose acceptance of the new creed was no more than half-hearted (which was the case for most) faced real peril if caught practicing ancestral rites. Spanish colonists competed with Franciscan friars to dominate American Indians. Both groups abused native tribes and exploited native labor.

The Pueblo revolt of 1680, in which American Indians burned churches, killed priests, and drove the Spanish out of New Mexico, taught the colonizers and priests to rethink their strategies. The priests' new approach, which was expanded to Texas and California during the 18th century, was more sensitive to native traditions. And they took notes from the French traders of the Great Lakes, Great Plains, and Louisiana Territory, who had more harmonious relationships with Indians.

Mission of Nuestra Señora de la Purisma Concepción, San Antonio, Texas. This mission was transferred from East Texas in 1731.

Instead of the rigid theological purity Franciscans had originally demanded, they now accepted American Indian rituals and celebrations incorporated into the already rich spectacle of Catholicism. They also winked at native parents' occasional backsliding, as long as they could teach orthodox doctrine to their sons and daughters. To this day, each pueblo celebrates the feast day of its patron saint with dances rooted in pre-Christian pagan beliefs.

Along with Christian dogma, priests taught the natives new farming techniques and crafts. Each mission was the center of what tried to be a self-sufficient community, with both agricultural workers and artisans, modeled as closely as possible on the essentially medieval peasant society of metropolitan Spain, but with a fortified compound at its heart. The church was the center, both geographically and temporally. Its bells (rather than the rhythms of nature) regulated the natives' lives, summoning them to prayer and to work and imposing a rigid religious, social, and moral discipline.

Many natives were unhappy about the enforced acculturation to an alien system. But the depredations of hostile attacks from other tribes and the demographic ravages of diseases imported from Europe left them little choice. The missions provided food, protection against raids, and a modicum of medical care. All they had to do in return was submit to the Spanish economic, cultural, and religious yoke. In the centuries that followed, the missions exerted a more positive influence.

Rosa's Window ("Rose Window"), Mission San José y San Miguel de Aguayo, San Antonio, Texas. This rose window demonstrates the high craftsmanship of artisans who worked on missions.

San Geronimo, Taos Pueblo, New Mexico. In 1620 a Spanish-Franciscan mission was established on the Taos River under the name of San Geronimo de Taos. The mission still exists, served by a priest, but the Taos people still practice old-time tribal rites.

JAMESTOWN
First Colony

JAMES CITY COUNTY, VIRGINIA

The London Company, holder of the royal charter for "southern Virginia" (which stretched from today's Carolinas to New York state), dispatched three ships—the *Susan Constant*, the *Godspeed*, and the *Discovery*—in December 1606. The 150 men on board—gentlemen, laborers, and craftsmen—were company employees, attracted by reports of the riches to be made in the New World. On May 13, 1607, the 105 survivors of the 16-week crossing landed on a semi-island sixty miles up the river (James River) and called their settlement Jamestown. Except for defensibility, it was a horrible location, short on fresh water and next to a swamp.

One by one, the men succumbed to disease, hunger, hostile attack, and intrigue. Capt. John Smith, a professional soldier hired by the Company to handle the colony's defense, soon emerged as its central figure. In December, he was captured by the natives and brought to their chief, Powhattan; this was the occasion of his famous encounter with the young Pocahontas. When allowed to return to Jamestown, in January, he found the thirty-eight surviving colonists about to embark for England. Later that same day, the situation was saved by the arrival of the first supply expedition, bringing food and new settlers.

Smith's arrangements with Powhattan kept the colony fed and secure until he was injured and forced to sail back to England in the fall of 1609. During the calamitous winter that followed, freezing weather, starvation, disease, and renewed attacks by the natives reduced the population from 500 to 60.

Susan Constant from Jamestown settlement, Colonial Williamsburg, Williamsburg, Virginia. This is a replica of one of the three ships that brought America's first English permanent colonists to Virginia in 1607.

On June 7, 1610, the survivors abandoned the settlement. They had gone only ten miles downstream when they met a boat sent ahead from the resupply fleet of Lord de la Warr, the new governor. The colony was reprieved.

The man who made it a success, however, was John Rolfe. He began growing tobacco in 1612 and married Pocahontas in 1614, initiating eight years of peace with the natives. Virginia tobacco, first sold in London in 1614, was an immediate success. Although disease and hostile natives slaughtered thousands during the next decade, the colony's survival was no longer in doubt.

Tobacco shaped Virginia. Its revenues made the colony viable. Its labor-intensive cultivation spurred the importation of black slaves. And its insatiable appetite for land ate away at the natives' holdings until Powhattan's people were subdued and confined to a reservation in 1651.

Jamestown served as the capital of the Virginia colony from 1607 to 1699. After the State House burned down for the fourth time, in 1698, the people of Williamsburg persuaded the legislature to relocate there. Jamestown, deprived of its *raison d'être*, was soon abandoned—this time forever. Only the brick church tower, built in 1639, remains.

Jamestown preceded Plymouth by thirteen years. John Smith and Pocahontas and John Rolfe are entrenched in the popular imagination more solidly than Miles

From 1607 to 1699, Jamestown was the capital of the Virginia colony. Virginia's first representative assembly met there in 1619.

Standish and John Alden and the fair Priscilla. But Plymouth, rather than Jamestown, is the founding legend of the United States, for several reasons.

The Pilgrims were a community that transplanted itself to the New World in search of freedom. The Jamestown settlers were hired hands, sent by the London Company and were eager to get rich.

In Jamestown, the first General Assembly was convened on instructions of the London Company, which retained ultimate control. Its first statute set a minimum price for tobacco. The Pilgrims, in the Mayflower Compact, established their own government. One of its first ordinances provided for jury trials in civil and criminal cases.

Many early Virginians returned to England when the opportunity presented itself, and Jamestown was nearly abandoned twice. In Plymouth, despite the terrible death toll of the first winter, no one sailed back to England with the *Mayflower* the following spring.

ABOVE: *Jamestown settlement, Colonial Williamsburg, Williamsburg, Virginia. This is a recreation of the early 17th century colonial fort.*
BELOW: *Ruins of a tavern, Jamestown.*

PLYMOUTH
Pilgrim Settlement

PLYMOUTH, MASSACHUSETTS

At the beginning of the 17th century, Europeans began landing on the coast of what is now New England. These adventurers alternately traded with, killed, and kidnapped the native Wampanoag. In 1616–1618, an epidemic killed more than 70% of the native population, who had no immunity to Old World viruses. Two years later, the survivors witnessed something new: Europeans, including women and children, debarked from their vessel and began to build permanent shelters on the site of Patuxet, a Wampanoag town of 2,000 people that had been abandoned after the plague.

The new immigrants centered around a group of Separatists who, having committed the treasonable act of rejecting the authority of the Church of England, fled to Holland in 1608. Unhappy in that tolerant country (where their children were learning to speak Dutch), they conceived the plan of colonizing the new land of "Virginia" across the ocean. They left the Netherlands on July 12 (old style), 1620, for Southampton, England, where they were joined by other Separatists.

Sixty-five of the 100 colonists at Plymouth were Pilgrims.

For various reasons, the *Mayflower* did not raise anchor until September 6; it was November 9 before its passengers sighted Cape Cod. Another month passed before they found a suitable location for their settlement. Late December was no time to begin a colony in the chilly climate of New England. (It was colder in the 17th century than today.) With inadequate food, inadequate shelter—inadequate everything except for faith in Divine Providence—half of the colonists and sailors did not survive the winter. At one point, only seven people were healthy enough to tend the sick. Despite the hardships, these Pilgrims persevered, laying out a street and installing cannon for defense.

In March, two English-speaking natives entered the village to reconnoiter the situation. Massasoit, the *sachem* of the Wampanoag, decided that the newcomers, with mysterious firearms, could be useful allies against rival tribes and came to their assistance.

The catastrophe of the first winter, when half of the colonists perished, was a test of their faith. As William Bradford noted in his journal of its founders' experiences, *Of Plimoth Plantation*, they viewed the Native American Squanto, who taught them survival skills when the winter was over, as "a special instrument sent of God for their good beyond their expectation." The first Thanksgiving

may have derived from the traditional English harvest festival. But nothing the Pilgrims did was isolated from their obligation to the Deity, so Thanksgiving could not avoid being a religious experience as well.

Our idea of the Pilgrims as a group that wanted to be left alone to follow their own unsullied course conforms to the American self-image as a people disdainfully turning away from the corruption of Europe. Their rejection of the traditional social and cultural order, with its rigid hierarchies, was amplified many times over in the pioneers who moved steadily westward in the 18th and 19th centuries.

This rock commemorates the Pilgrims landing at Plymouth (Plimoth) in 1620.

Plymouth Rock Memorial State Park, Plymouth, Massachusetts. The Pilgrims landed and established a settlement in the New World, helping define religious freedom as well as the just and equal laws we all value today.

Two days after landfall, the colonists drew up the Mayflower Compact. Basing themselves on the forms of governance of their church, they agreed to establish a "civil Body Politick" "for our better ordering and preservation...to enact, constitute and frame...just and equal laws." Here we have the social contract of English political theory, decades before it was formulated with similar clarity in the mother country and 150 years before it inspired Jefferson and his colleagues to assert that legitimate government is created by and rests on the consent of the governed.

Thus the American nation, which grounded its government on "we, the people" and adopted "in God we trust" as its motto, can, like many of its citizens, trace its antecedents to those who came over on the *Mayflower*.

The short-lived Dominion of New England, dating from 1688 and of which Plymouth had been a part, was absorbed by the Massachusetts Bay Colony in 1691.

SALEM

Witchcraft Trials

"What evil spirit have you familiarity with?"—"None."
"Have you made no contract with the devil?"—"No."
"Why do you hurt these children?"—"I do not hurt them. I scorn it."
"Who do you imploy then to do it?"—"I imploy no body."
"What creature do you imploy then?"—"No creature. I am falsely accused."

—Judges John Hathorne and Jonathan Corwin examining Sarah Good, *The Salem Witchcraft Papers*, Book II

DANVERS AND SALEM, MASSACHUSETTS

To people in the 17th century, the Devil was just as real as the man next door. What is more, unlike God, he had direct relations with human beings. Even reputable scientists allowed that some phenomena were caused by witchcraft. Because Satan posed a grave threat to the social and political order, his minions were subversives; in 1641 Parliament made witchcraft a capital offense. From time to time witches were hanged in England and its colonies (three in Massachusetts before 1692). But there was never anything like the madness that overtook Salem Village (modern Danvers) in 1692.

In 1688, 13-year-old Martha Goodwin of Boston and three of her siblings fell ill. Their physician concluded that "hellish witchcraft" was the only possible cause. Martha accused the family's Irish housekeeper, Goody Glover. The Reverend Cotton Mather, who examined both Glover and Martha, denounced Glover at her trial as "scandalous, poor, a Roman Catholic, and obstinate in idolatry." Glover was hanged. Mather's published analysis of the affair, with graphic accounts of the children's contortions, became a bestseller throughout Massachusetts.

In January 1692, the daughter and niece of the Reverend Samuel Parris of Salem Village, aged nine and eleven, began behaving strangely. Soon other Salem girls were acting similarly. The local doctor, all his nostrums in vain, blamed witchcraft. Pressed to identify their tormentors, Elizabeth Parris named Tituba, her family's South American Indian slave, and two social misfits, Sarah Good and Sarah Osborne. Good and Osborne denied the charge, but Tituba, succumbing to psychological and physical pressure, confessed and incriminated them.

During the coming weeks, a long list of villagers, both children and adults, implicated other residents. Relatives and friends who came to the defense of the accused found themselves arraigned on the same charges. In late May, with dozens of persons in custody, the newly arrived governor of the colony empanelled a special court to try their cases.

The court sat until September, its juries handing down dozens of guilty verdicts and few acquittals, because the "victims'" testimony was deemed incontrovertible. In the warped logic of that nightmare, reinforced by the Puritan penchant for confession

Burying Point, Salem, Massachusetts. This is the oldest burying ground in the city of Salem. Buried here is Justice John Hathorne, a judge in the Witchcraft Court and an ancestor of Nathaniel Hawthorne (who added a "w" to his name to distance himself from his forebear).

Salem Witch Trial Memorial, Salem, Massachusetts. Dedicated in 1992, at the 300th anniversary, to commemorate the victims of the Salem witch trials of 1692.

and repentance, those who confessed were spared, while those who steadfastly maintained their innocence were *ipso facto* guilty and ended on the gallows. Ultimately, 19 men and women were hanged, one man was crushed to death for refusing to enter a plea, and others died in prison.

Many citizens were uneasy, but few spoke out. It was not until early October that two prominent Bostonians—Increase Mather, Cotton's father and the president of Harvard College, and wealthy merchant Thomas Brattle—published demonstrations of the rational absurdity of the proceedings. Before the month was over, the governor dissolved the special court. All the remaining prisoners were released or pardoned the next year.

In 1697, a troubled Massachusetts General Court ordered a day of fasting and introspection. In 1702, it declared the trials unlawful. In 1706, one of the principal accusers stood up in church, her head bowed, while the preacher read out her admission that she had spoken untruthfully and caused the deaths of innocent people. In 1711, legislation restored the victims' rights and reputations and paid substantial compensation to their heirs.

New England Puritanism never recovered its former influence and reputation. But the protracted soul-searching, confession, and restitution are evidence of its positive core—humble acknowledgment of one's own imperfections. Brattle was afraid that "ages will not wear off that reproach and those stains which these things will leave behind them upon our land." In fact, by their Puritan contrition the people of Massachusetts did much to lighten those stains. In the end, they were not too proud to stand up and agree with Martha Carrier, hanged on August 19, 1692: "I am wronged. It is a shameful thing that you should mind these folks that are out of their wits."

NEW ENGLAND PORTS
Shipbuilding & Trading

MASSACHUSETTS, NEW HAMPSHIRE, RHODE ISLAND, CONNECTICUT, AND MAINE PORTS

No one ever got rich through agriculture in New England, with its poor and stony soil, mountainous terrain, cold winters, and short growing season. Instead, those with initiative turned to the sea—initially to fishing and whaling and then to international trade. The one natural resource with which the country was abundantly endowed was timber, so New England built ships and sailed them all over the world. By the end of the colonial period, one-third of all vessels flying the British flag were built in New England.

The ship Friendship *in the port of Salem, Massachusetts.*

Today we associate Salem with witches, which is unfair, because the Salem Village of the late 17th century was distinct from the port of Salem Town. In fact, Salem Town, founded as a fishing village in 1626 (four years before Boston), was long the second port of New England. Along with Boston and other, smaller ports, by the middle of the 17th century it had developed a lucrative trade with the West Indies, in which salt cod was a major item, thanks to British laws that gave the American colonies a virtual monopoly on that trade.

The first kind of international commerce that brought true prosperity to North American merchants was the "triangular trade." Ships sailed from American ports with a cargo of locally distilled rum, which they traded for slaves in West Africa. The unfortunate Africans were then carried to the West Indies, where the sugar planters paid for them with molasses produced from their cane. The molasses was taken back to New England, where it was turned into rum. And then the cycle began again.

New England lived well off this business until new duties and trade restrictions imposed by Parliament to pay for the cost of defending the colonies against the French and Indians cut into their profits. Hell hath no fury like a merchant whose purse is pinched by the government—which is why merchant shipowners like John Hancock were among the prime movers and financial backers of the Revolution.

The Revolutionary War put a stop to this trade. Encouraged by Congress, which was unable to build a large navy quickly, many shipowners turned to privateering and preyed on British merchant ships. This created several fortunes, including those of the Cabots and Lowells. During the Revolution, Salem provided more privateers (158) than any other port.

Deprived of the trade benefits it had enjoyed under the protection of the British crown, the New England economy stagnated after the war. Left with their privateering vessels, which were too large for the coasting trade, the merchants expanded their horizons and began doing business with China, India, Russia, and the East Indies, dealing in luxury goods like tea, coffee, pepper, and Indian textiles. One of the pioneers of this trade, shipowner Elias Hasket Derby of Salem (who never went to sea in his life), became the richest man in America. In 1790, Salem, with a population of around 8,000, was the seventh largest city in the U.S. and probably the richest per capita. The three decades between the Revolution and 1812, when it gained international fame as the "Venice of the New World," were its heyday. The Embargo of 1807 ended this prosperity. Salem never recovered, though during the War of 1812 it again provided one-sixth of all American privateers.

These merchants, the first capitalists in the New World, provided the spark for the future economic development of the country by investing their profits in industry (which in those days meant textiles), real estate, and banking. Later they provided much of the seed money for the first railroads.

NANTUCKET
Whaling & Fishing

"The spermacetti whale found by the Nantuckois, is an active, fierce animal, and requires vast address and boldness in the fishermen."—Thomas Jefferson to the French minister, 1778

NANTUCKET, MASSACHUSETTS (ISLAND OFF CAPE COD)

North American colonists began organized whaling as early as 1640, on Long Island. This shore-based industry, applying European techniques, expanded to New Jersey and New England by the end of the century.

In the 18th century, with fewer cetaceans swimming close to shore, whalers turned to deep-water voyages that might last for several weeks. But they still brought the blubber back to shore to extract the oil. Later, as the market for whale products expanded and the sperm whale replaced the right whale as the preferred prey, true deep-sea whaling began, first in the open Atlantic and later in the Indian and Pacific Oceans. On these long voyages the ships became factories and the crew extracted the oil on deck.

Before the Revolution, more than 350 whaling vessels were sailing from ports in New York and New England. The almost unbroken succession of hostilities in the next four decades (Revolutionary War, Napoleonic Wars, War of 1812) left the industry in a depressed state.

The Golden Age of American whaling began in 1815. During the next 40 years, the fleet grew to more than 700 vessels sailing from 23 ports. Whaling was a filthy and dangerous pursuit, but it offered adventure and fantastic profits. What is more, at a time when America was an international backwater, it was one branch of endeavor in which all acknowledged that the New Englanders were unsurpassed.

The two most important whaling ports were New Bedford, on the mainland, and Nantucket, an island 24 miles south of Cape Cod. At its peak, in 1857, New Bedford alone was the home port of 329 whaleships, whose crews numbered 10,000 men of many polyglot races—Yankee country boys, Portuguese islanders, Native Americans from Martha's Vineyard, and South Sea islanders.

Brant Point Lighthouse, Nantucket Island, Massachusetts. Erected in 1746, this was the second lighthouse built in America.

This unique world was immortalized by Herman Melville in *Moby Dick*. Melville, who had himself signed aboard the New Bedford whaleship *Acushnet* in December 1840, combined his experiences on that vessel with the true account of the sinking of a whaleship by an enraged cetacean some years earlier to produce one of the masterpieces of American prose. The ballast of factual information and whaling lore that provides weight and stability to his tale of the *Pequod*'s voyage is an important source of what the modern world knows about that business. Melville's literary reputation did not last, however; for decades his masterwork lay sunk in oblivion, much like the *Pequod* itself.

The demand for whale oil for illumination plummeted after petroleum was discovered in Pennsylvania in 1859. Then the Civil War decimated the fleet. After the war the industry, now focused in the North Pacific, continued because baleen, which noncarnivorous whales have instead of teeth, proved to be the best material for parts and products that required elasticity—carriage springs, corset stays, fishing rods, and so on. The invention of spring steel in 1906 ended the market for baleen. The last American whalers were retired in the 1920s—just around the time that scholars and the general public rediscovered *Moby Dick*.

"So be cheery, my lads, let your hearts never fail,
While the bold harpooner is striking the whale!"
—Nantucket Song

Nantucket Harbor, Nantucket Island, Massachusetts. Nantucket was an early whaling and fishing center.

GREAT LAKES
Fur Trade & Industrial Waterway

LAKES SUPERIOR, MICHIGAN, HURON, ERIE, AND ONTARIO

About 10,000 years ago, the Wisconsin Ice Age created the Great Lakes, the most prominent feature on the United States map, that also defines America's northern border with Canada. The Great Lakes—Superior, Michigan, Huron, Erie, and Ontario—hold one-fifth of the world's fresh surface water. They have a combined surface area of about 95,000 square miles and drain a watershed of about 295,000 square miles. The Straits of Mackinac, St. Marys River, St. Clair River, Detroit River, and Niagara River, and the 460-square-mile Lake St. Clair link the Great Lakes. From Duluth, Minnesota, on western Lake Superior, to Lake Ontario's outlet on the St. Lawrence River is a distance of 1,160 miles. Michigan's shoreline alone runs 3,200 miles—longer than that of the entire Eastern seaboard.

Sandy beaches and dunes, cattail marshes, limestone cliffs, safe harbors, and busy ports hug the Great Lakes. Volcanic eruptions below ancient seas deposited copper, iron, silver, gold, gypsum, and dolomite. Lands surrounding the Great Lakes boast salt beds, fertile soils, rich harvests, dense forests, fur-bearing animals, and more species of bird than anywhere else in North America (Point Pelee, Ontario). Easy transport of raw materials and finished goods on the Great Lakes spurred growth of the Midwest's grain, timber, rail, shipping, construction, and manufacturing industries. A freighter hauls iron ore mined from Michigan's upper peninsula (the U.P.) south through Lake Huron to Lake Erie and a Cleveland foundry where it is refined, rolled into sheets, and shipped to Chicago on Lake Michigan or to Detroit on the Detroit River to be shaped into steel girders, rails, auto parts, ship hulls, tools, and other goods.

An Old Copper Culture thrived some 7,000 years ago on Lake Superior's Isle Royale and the Keweenaw Peninsula in Michigan's U.P. and traded pure, high-grade copper tools and utensils with other tribes who took these goods as far south as the Gulf of Mexico. Early Mound Builders, the Adena, arrived 3,000 years ago, and the Hopewell, architects of complex mounds, a little later. Later the Five Nations of the Iroquois drove the Algonquian-speaking tribes into the Great Lakes and Ohio Valley. The Algonquians pushed the Sioux onto the Great Plains.

French and British colonists found the Three Fires, a highly developed and competitive Algonquian-speaking confederation—the Potawatomi, Ottawa, and Chippewa (Ojibwa). The Potawatomi built elaborate villages near Lake Michigan and cultivated beans, corn, and squash. The Ottawa grew crops but moved their villages during fishing season. The nomadic Chippewa hunted, fished, and gathered berries and fruit in the far north. The Fox, Sauk, Miami, Wyandot, and remnants of

Opened in 1957, the 5-mile (26,372-feet) Mackinac Bridge spans the Straits of Mackinac between Lake Michigan and Lake Huron, and connects Michigan's upper and lower peninsulas. It is the longest suspension bridge in the western hemisphere. The length of its greatest suspension, including anchorages, is 8,614 feet, and the total length of wire in the cables is 42,000 miles. Maximum water depth at midspan is 295 feet. Signs posted at the bridge's entrance warn motorists of high winds and adverse weather. © Corbis.

Lands around the Great Lakes do not experience the same temperature extremes as the upper Midwest and upper Great Plains. The semi-maritime climate of the Great Lakes states means lake-effect cooling in summer and warming in winter, and an average 10-degree temperature moderation compared with the inland.

the Hurons lived in the region. Dugout canoes made from hollowed-out logs were later replaced by lightweight, swift, and easy-to-maneuver birch-bark canoes devised by Algonquian-speaking tribes.

The first Europeans who explored the Great Lakes were searching for the Northwest Passage to the Pacific Ocean and China, with its promise of rich silks, spices, porcelain, gold, and precious stones. Samuel de Champlain, lieutenant governor of New France, ordered Jean Nicolet in 1634 to explore lands west of Quebec. Landing at Green Bay, Nicolet donned his imperial robes and greeted the astonished Winnebago. Without sailing to the Far East, Champlain grew rich on the fur trade and the beaver hats demanded by fashionable Europeans. The Three Fires nation, ancient traders, readily accepted the Frenchmen's knives, beads, blankets, iron kettles, trinkets, guns, and whiskey in exchange for fur pelts. The French constructed forts at the Straits of Mackinac, Detroit, St. Joseph, and Sault Ste. Marie to protect fur traders from the ancient Indian practice of raiding. French voyageurs loaded large multiple-oared birch-bark canoes and swiftly transported furs hundreds of miles, while singing and paddling in rhythm.

The British were less successful in the fur trade; Sir William Johnson demanded in 1764 that all transactions be at Detroit and Mackinac. As a result traders from New York, Montreal, and beyond the Mississippi captured the market. Fur pelt exports declined from 1764 to 1768 from 28,067 to 18,923 British pounds sterling. After the Civil War, the fur trade waned.

The opening of the Erie Canal in 1825 and the Ilinois and Michigan Canal in 1848 increased Great Lakes traffic. Settlers in steel-hulled steamers that replaced sailing ships found their way west or settled in shipping ports or along banks. At lakeside sawmill sites, timber cut from dense woodlands surrounding the Great Lakes were shipped down the Mississippi or the Hudson to build American towns and cities.

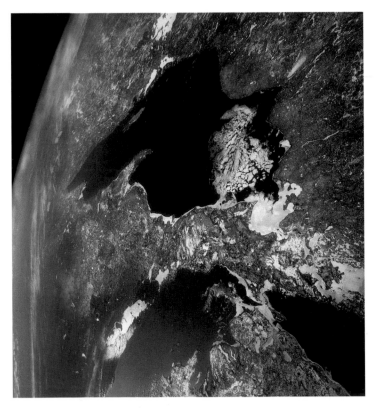

Completion of the Sault Ste. Marie Canals (U.S. 1855 and Canadian 1895), Welland Ship Canal (1829 and 1932), and the St. Lawrence Seaway (1959) made it possible to accommodate ocean-going vessels up to 740 and 1,000 feet. The route from Southampton, England, to Detroit is shorter than that from Southampton to Baltimore. Steamers, tug-and-barge units, self-propelled lakers, and freighters haul billions of tons of foodstuffs, metal, tools, and lumber to distant ports. The U.S.-flag fleet's thirteen 1,000-foot self-unloading freighters are able to discharge 65,000 tons of iron ore, coal, or limestone within 10 hours without shore assistance. Cement, salt, sand, grain, and liquid-bulk products are other major cargoes. Major industrial centers and ports Cleveland, Detroit, Chicago, Milwaukee, Green Bay, Duluth, Toledo, Erie, and Buffalo thrive on active lake commerce, halted only by winter ice.

Lake Superior and the upper parts of Lake Michigan and Lake Huron, viewed from space. Winter ice, shown here, can make large sections of the Great Lakes impassable. Lake Superior sometimes behaves like an ocean with giant waves, 100-foot seiches, and sudden, dramatic storms, such as the one that sank the S.S. Edmund Fitzgerald in 1975. © Corbis.

FORT TICONDEROGA
The French & Indian Wars to the American Revolution

"Surrender in the name of the great Jehovah and the Continental Congress!"
—Ethan Allen and the Green Mountain Boys to the British commander of Fort Ticonderoga, May 10, 1775

TICONDEROGA, NEW YORK

Except for Washington—who lost more battles than he won and whose success lay in keeping his army intact and the British bottled up on the coast—the Revolutionary War general who contributed the most to the colonies' victory was none other than Benedict Arnold.

The bravest and most brilliant American commander in the war, he first distinguished himself at Ticonderoga and during the ill-fated invasion of Canada in 1775. His holding action at the Battle of Valcour (October 1776) delayed the British penetration of the Hudson Valley by an entire year, giving the Continental Army time to organize. Finally, his bold leadership at the two battles of Saratoga (September–October 1777) frustrated the British plan to sever New England from the middle colonies and forced Gen. Burgoyne to surrender—which in turn led directly to the French decision to conclude an alliance with the struggling United States. It was *the* turning point of the war.

Fort Ticonderoga, New York. The French & Indian War (1754–1763) helped create the soldiers of the American Revolution.

Lake Champlain in upstate New York as seen from Fort Ticonderoga.

Fort Ticonderoga, on a peninsula between Lake George and Lake Champlain, about 100 miles north of Albany, began as a quickly constructed French fortification, Fort Carillon, during the French and Indian War. In 1758, the French scored their only major victory of that war when Montcalm's small garrison repulsed an onslaught by a British force five times as large. But the French tenure in Carillon was temporary. The next year the garrison withdrew in the face of superior British forces, who rebuilt it as "Ticonderoga," from an Iroquois word meaning "place between two waters."

Sixteen years later, fired by the news of Lexington and Concord, Arnold, a militia captain from New Haven, marched his men toward Boston. He persuaded the Massachusetts Committee of Safety—the rebel provisional government of the colony—to support an attack on Ticonderoga, noting that its cannon could then be hauled to Boston to threaten the British forces occupying the town. (The cannon arrived in January 1776 and contributed to the British decision to evacuate the city.) Commissioned a colonel, he hurried westward, only to encounter Ethan Allen and his Green Mountain Boys—a guerrilla force originally set up to contest New York's claim to Vermont.

Allen, who at 37 was three years older than Arnold, also had a New Haven connection, having been educated at Yale. Arnold had the commission, but Allen had the local troops and led the assault. In the predawn hours of May 10, 1775, in the colonists' first offensive action of the war, Allen and his 80 men walked through the open gate and overpowered the sleeping sentry. Allen blustered, Arnold asked politely, and the 48-man garrison surrendered without firing a shot.

The Continental Congress, appalled at this first offensive strike of the war, wanted the fort abandoned, but the New England provincial assemblies demurred. In July 1777, however, the American forces fled as Burgoyne's army approached. After Burgoyne's surrender at Saratoga in November, the British garrison torched

the Ticonderoga fortifications and withdrew. After a brief but eventful history of two decades, during which it was attacked six times but never fell to direct assault, Ticonderoga returned to obscurity, its stonework hauled away by local farmers. Only in 1909 was it restored.

In Allen's highly entertaining account of the capture of Ticonderoga, ornamented by his claim that he had demanded its surrender in the name of "the Great Jehovah and the Continental Congress," Arnold has been totally written out. His failure to receive credit for his exploits was a continuing irritation to this proud and irascible man. Gen. Horatio Gates, the American commander at Saratoga, did not even mention him in his dispatches. Washington appreciated his military genius, but Congress never treated him fairly. It was these repeated slights to his honor, which began with Ticonderoga, that started him on his tragic road to treason and infamy.

Fort Ticonderoga, Ticonderoga, New York.

FARMS

Growing Food for America's Tables

"This is a place where you can hear fall coming for miles."—Charles Kuralt on Horicon Marsh in Wisconsin, 1986

RURAL AMERICA

The Mississippian Mound Builders grew various native crops. Later they began to cultivate maize, domesticated in Meso-America around A.D. 800–1100. By producing food surpluses, this superior cereal remade their culture into a centralized society with large urban centers; Cahokia at its peak had a population of 20,000. But climatic change, political instability, and European diseases destroyed this civilization by the 16th century.

The Spanish introduced cattle and horses. Other species of domesticated livestock were brought to the New World in the 17th and 18th centuries. The early European settlers borrowed many crops from the natives, including maize, sweet potatoes, and pumpkins, while bringing with them the major cereals and dozens of varieties of fruits and vegetables.

Labor was expensive in colonial America, so most farmers relied on family members. Land, however, was cheap and seemingly inexhaustible. When yields declined, farmers could simply move farther west. Most did not view subsistence or self-sufficiency as their goal; what they wanted was the higher standard of living that only cash crops could bring.

Tobacco was the first staple to command so high a price that farmers stopped growing their own food. Eventually, monoculture came to dominate the South—rice, sugarcane, and especially cotton. These plantation crops were labor-intensive and could be produced more profitably using gangs of slaves.

The switch from hand- to horsepower, between 1830 and 1875, was the first American agricultural revolution. The production of basic commodities like wheat and corn skyrocketed between 1860 and 1890, making it possible to feed the rapidly increasing urban population. But their growing dependence on factory-made machinery

> Agricultural machinery changed farming. The cast-iron plow (1819), steel plow (1839), and reaper (1834), mowing machines, cultivators, and mechanical threshers increased crop yields and reduced farmers' labor.
>
> Between 1830 and 1860, yields of staple crops, such as corn, wheat, cotton, tobacco, and wool, doubled. The West came to dominate in grain production and livestock. New England farmers turned to truck gardens and dairies, as well as raising livestock.

Farm, Racine County, Wisconsin.

Farm in northwest Wyoming, near Montana. The centuries-old agrarian myth has depicted bucolic comforts seldom realized on the modest family farm. Many early settlers had difficulty growing enough to feed themselves and to bring crops to market.

and a single crop increased farmers' need for cash and credit and locked them into an unbreakable cycle of debt, at the mercy of bankers and suppliers.

Their distress and anger fueled the Populist Party of the 1890s. Although the party did well in the West and South, it was never able to shape national policy. Nevertheless, the Populist credo that industry and commerce were corrupt and corrupting, and had brought the country to "the verge of moral, political, and material ruin," struck a resonant chord. The fountainhead of the adulation of agrarian life was Thomas Jefferson, who had viewed the independent farmer as the embodiment of morality and the bedrock of republican government. He believed that a broad smallholder class, each family owning its own means of production and relying on its own labor, was the best guarantee that the evils of Europe, urban and feudal, would not spread to the New World.

But Jefferson himself was a plantation owner, not a yeoman farmer. Plantation agriculture retarded the growth of a merchant and artisan class, discouraged non-land investments, and kept towns from developing—paradoxically giving the appearance of the agrarian ideal far more than true smallholdings did.

Even after they traded self-sufficiency for a higher standard of living, smallholders found that the amenities of life on the family farm remained sparse. In 1930, only 34% of U.S. farms had telephones and only 13% electricity. Largely thanks to the Rural Electrification Act of 1936, between one-fourth and one-third had electricity by 1940. Even then, however, only 8.5% of farm homes had flush toilets (95% of urban homes did). Nearly full electrification was not achieved until the late 1960s.

By the late 20th century, idealized self-sufficient family farms with neat barns and docile cows had long since been replaced by agribusiness corporations who even patented the seeds farmers planted. Even so, the longing for a simpler agrarian past with what we imagine to be a solid moral center refuses to vanish from the American mind. Few farmers, although they have maintained a strong social, economic, and political voice, have remained independent of government involvement, regulatory or financial. Farmers' sons and daughters have found other occupations. Agrarian virtues have not kept them down on the farm after seeing the lights of the city.

POPULATION OF FARMERS According to the United States Department of Agriculture, in 1790, farmers made up about 90% of the labor force and by 1840 that figure had dropped to 69%. In 1870 farmers made up 53% of the labor force, by 1900 38%. The numbers continued to decline with each decade of the 20th century. In 1950, farmers were 12.2% of the labor force.

In 1990 when 246,081,000 people lived in the United States, 4,591,000 were farmers, just 2.6% of the labor force. In 1990, the average farm was 461 acres and the number of farms 2,143,150.

In the colonies, *Poor Richard's Almanack* (1732–1758) offered agricultural predictions, charts of the moon's phases, and Benjamin Franklin's entertaining remarks: "A countryman between two lawyers is like a fish between two cats."

In the 1820s, agricultural periodicals began to express farmers' political issues. The Morrill Land Grant College Act of 1862 helped states establish land-grant colleges with agriculture and mechanical arts curricula.

OLD STATE HOUSE
Open Debate in Colony & Commonwealth

BOSTON, MASSACHUSETTS

In an era of satellite reception and C-span, we take the public nature of legislative deliberations for granted (and think it rather quaint that the Supreme Court still excludes cameras). But it was not until 1766–1767, when a visitors' gallery was built in the Representatives' Hall of the Old State House in Boston, that citizens were able to monitor debates of their elected representatives. This innovation was a natural for Massachusetts, whose original settlers had honed the tradition of self-government in their churches, where only piety, age, and eloquence counted and every congregant could be heard.

What is now called the Old State House was originally constructed in 1712–1713 on the site of the former Boston Town Hall, which had burned down in 1711. Substantially rebuilt after a fire in 1743, it served as the seat of government for the colony and then the Commonwealth of Massachusetts until the current State House was dedicated in 1798.

The State House was the center of government, but the Customs House, which stood across the way, was of equal if not greater importance for British colonial interests. After British troops were posted to Boston in 1768 to quell the unrest sparked by the colonists' resentment of various taxes, duties, and legislation that restricted commerce, a guard stood outside the building at all times. On Monday evening, March 5, 1770, an unruly crowd of 30 to 60 men and boys began taunting him. The officer of the day, after much hesitation, came to defend him with a small squad of soldiers. The mob hurled snowballs and other objects at the soldiers and continued their insults. At some point one of the British soldiers fired at his assailants. Within minutes, four colonials were dead and another lay mortally wounded.

The Patriot party, led by Sam Adams, immediately turned this unfortunate incident into a "massacre" and whipped public opinion into an anti-British frenzy. Employing the threat of more unrest, Adams and John Hancock coerced Governor Thomas Hutchinson to withdraw the troops from the city. No doubt this victory emboldened the colonists when the struggle for independence began five years later.

The soldiers were put on trial, since Massachusetts law forbade them to open fire except at the direct order of a civil magistrate. The governor delayed the trial for six months, to allow passions to cool. John Adams, Sam Adams' second cousin and no Loyalist, agreed to defend them, believing that the facts of the case were on their side. He won acquittal for the officer and later for all the soldiers except the two who had undoubtedly discharged their weapons (found guilty of manslaughter, not murder, they walked free by invoking benefit of clergy, a relic of the Middle Ages that had in effect exempted the literate from capital punishment). In his old age, John Adams said that his defense of the soldiers had been "one of the most gallant, generous, manly, and disinterested actions of my whole life, and one of the best pieces of service I ever rendered my country," by standing up for the rule of law against mob rule.

The Old State House in Boston, Massachusetts.

OLD NORTH CHURCH

"The Redcoats Are Coming!"

BOSTON, MASSACHUSETTS

The Old North Church, officially the Episcopal "Christ Church in the City of Boston," constructed in 1723, is Boston's oldest surviving church building. It earned its niche in American history on the night of April 18–19, 1775, when sexton Robert Newman hung two lanterns in its steeple, informing Paul Revere and other patriot riders that the British forces were moving by sea.

Following the Boston Tea Party, the British had closed the port of Boston and appointed Gen. Thomas Gage governor and military commander of the rebellious province, with a beefed-up garrison in Boston. Gage sent his troops on occasional forays into the countryside, but King George III of England was not satisfied with the results. In April, Gage decided to seize rebel stores in Lexington and Concord and arrest John Hancock and Samuel Adams, the leading radicals. To give their horseback couriers a head start on the Redcoats so that they could alert the countryside, patriot spies in Boston arranged for lanterns to be hung in the North Church steeple, the tallest in town—one if the Redcoats left Boston by the land route, two if they crossed Boston Harbor to take the shorter route through Charlestown.

Revere and other riders fanned out through the countryside. The alerted colonial militias—the Minutemen—were waiting for the Redcoats at Lexington. A shot rang out. Soon eight Americans lay dead on the green.

Paul Revere Statue and Old North Church Steeple. The celebrated Paul Revere, a silversmith, was only one of many night riders and patriots who warned the citizenry of the British approach.

The British marched on to Concord, where the Minutemen fired a series of deadly volleys and barred their path across the bridge. The bloodied Redcoats began a disorderly retreat to Boston, with the colonials sniping at them from behind trees and fences.

Another courier, Israel Bissel, galloped off to Worcester and then to Connecticut with the news of Lexington even before the British began their retreat from Concord. The news galvanized the population into action. Although colonists had fought against French and Indians on the frontier, it had been generations since there had been an assault on their homes and families in settled districts. Within days, militiamen from all over New England had assembled in Cambridge, pinning the British in Boston. There could be no turning back from armed rebellion now.

The lanterns in the church steeple really should be no more than a footnote. American history would not have been substantially different had the British captured and hanged Hancock and Adams. The lanterns have shone so brightly through the generations and become one of the best-known details of the colonists' fight for independence because of Paul Revere's memoirs and Henry Wadsworth Longfellow's versification of that one brief incident in Revere's long and eventful life.

North Bridge, Minute Man National Historic Park, Concord, Massachusetts.

Longfellow was one of the first writers to find poetic inspiration in the history and landscape of America. In an age when poems and ballads were as popular and influential as movies are today, his retelling of a piquant episode from the early history of the Plymouth Colony in "The Courtship of Miles Standish," his haunting account of a young woman's quest through the wild frontier for her betrothed in "Evangeline," the sonorous lines and pulsing rhythms of a romantic evocation of Native Americans in "Song of Hiawatha," and "The Midnight Ride of Paul Revere" became primary texts from which Americans learned their history.

Two generations after the night riders, Ralph Waldo Emerson's "Concord Hymn" immortalized the "shot heard round the world." Although resistance at Concord did wonders for colonists' morale and excited European imaginations, for the patriots of 1775, the deaths on Lexington Green set the colonies on their inexorable course toward independence. That June, when pioneers in central Kentucky wanted to give suitable expression to their patriotic fervor, they named the new settlement not Concord, but Lexington.

Listen, my children, and you shall hear
Of the midnight ride of Paul Revere,
On the 18th of April, in Seventy-five;
Hardly a man is now alive
Who remembers that famous day and year.

He said to his friend, "If the British march
By land or sea from the town to-night,
Hang a lantern aloft in the belfry arch
Of the North Church tower as a signal light,—
One, if by land, and two, if by sea;
And I on the opposite shore will be,
Ready to ride and spread the alarm
Through every Middlesex village and farm
For the country folk to be up and to arm."

—from Henry Wadsworth Longfellow's poem "Paul Revere's Ride"

BUNKER HILL

First Major Battle of the American Revolution

"Don't one of you fire until you see the whites of their eyes."—William Prescott, June 17, 1775

BOSTON, MASSACHUSETTS

It was a battle fought on the wrong hill by largely untrained men who had no idea, when they were mustered the day before, that they would soon be facing the most professional fighting force in the world. For the latter, it was a battle fought using inappropriate tactics, on ground of the enemy's choosing, surrounded by hostile and rebellious civilians. The professionals were left in possession of the field and thought they had won. But Bunker Hill was the first battle also fought in the arena of what we now call PR (public relations); from that perspective, it was the routed defenders who won the day.

In the early summer of 1775, the British army controlled Boston. But its writ did not even extend to Cambridge, on the other side of the Charles River, and the hinterland was firmly in the hands of the rebellious colonists. Since their ill-fated excursion to Lexington and Concord in April, the British had been preparing a major effort to break out of their encirclement. Their generals were confident that the ragtag militia of farmers, mechanics, and merchants was no match for their highly trained soldiers. They expected that a few harsh defeats would take the wind out of the rebels' sails, encourage loyalists to rally to the cause, and bring the insurrection to a speedy end.

The Bunker Hill Monument is located on Breed's Hill, site of the first major battle of the American Revolution. Although the colonists lost the battle, their bravery against the British encouraged them to continue to fight.

The colonists resolved to forestall this scenario. On June 16, 1775, about a thousand men from Massachusetts and Connecticut, commanded by Col. William Prescott, were summoned to a review on Cambridge Commons. At its conclusion they were ordered to march to the Charlestown peninsula and prepare a defensive position for an imminent battle.

Prescott had been told to fortify Bunker Hill, the highest in the vicinity, but he and his officers decided on the lower Breed's Hill instead. Starting at midnight, working as quietly as possible, the men dug, chopped, and raised protective breastworks.

At dawn, British sailors saw what was happening and opened fire on the still incomplete fortifications, but they were out of range. The colonials continued working feverishly; they gained a few more hours because the tide kept the British from ferrying troops across the harbor until 1 p.m. After halting to rest and eat, the Redcoats began their uphill attack—more than 2,000 well-armed soldiers against half as many defenders with limited ammunition. Whether or not Prescott really told his men, "Don't fire until you see the whites of their eyes," that is what they did. When the advancing British finally came within range of their muskets, they let go with a murderous volley. The Redcoats broke—twice.

Freedom Trail logo. Bunker Hill and other sites of the American Revolution can be found along Boston's Freedom Trail.

The third British charge, against colonials down to their last few bullets, carried the breastworks. In the hand-to-hand combat that ensued, casualties were high on both sides. The militiamen withdrew to Cambridge as best they could.

The British were left in possession of the two hills, having suffered more than 200 dead and more than 800 wounded (almost 50% of the troops committed). On the colonial side, 115 were killed and 305 wounded.

The British consoled themselves that they had won the battle—although, in the words of Maj. Gen. Henry Clinton, "another such [victory] would have ruined us."

A broadside published in Philadelphia a week later reported that the militia had almost gained "a compleat victory." In terms of morale, it was: the colonists had faced a superior British force in pitched battle and shown themselves equal to the challenge. It would be a difficult struggle, they realized, but victory was conceivable. The British, for their part, woke up to the possibility of defeat. Thus the misnamed Battle of Bunker Hill first brought home to both sides that the rebellion sparked by a few fanatic Bostonians might also be misnamed; it was really an American Revolution.

Two weeks later, George Washington assumed command at Cambridge and began to whip the 15,000 undisciplined militiamen into an army.

The Bunker Hill granite obelisk stands 221 feet tall. The bronze statue, made in 1881 by William W. Story, is that of Col. William Prescott.

VALLEY FORGE

Washington's Continental Army Camp

"To see the men without clothes to cover their nakedness, without blankets to lie upon, without shoes...without a house or hut to cover them until those could be built, and submitting without a murmur, is a proof of patience and obedience which, in my opinion, can scarcely be paralleled."—George Washington at Valley Forge, April 21, 1778

VALLEY FORGE, PENNSYLVANIA

The best-remembered site associated with the Revolutionary War is not a battlefield, the scene of martial bravery. It is rather Valley Forge, where the Continental Army encamped during the winter of 1777–1778, that has become the emblem of that struggle.

Artillery barrages, musket fire, and bayonet charges may have been absent, but there was no shortage of suffering. In the six months from December 19, 1777, when the troops (some 10,000 to 12,000) began arriving at the site, to June 9, 1778, when they moved out, between 2,000 and 3,000 soldiers succumbed to hunger, disease, and the elements.

The fortunes of the fledgling United States were at low ebb. The British had a firm grip on New York City. In the wake of Washington's defeats at Brandywine and Germantown, Philadelphia, capital of the infant country, had fallen to Gen. William Howe's Redcoats. Congress fled to Lancaster and then to York.

Washington's strategic decision, at this fateful juncture, could be described as "showing the flag." Valley Forge was a defensible position, close enough to Philadelphia to keep the British on their toes and Patriot morale from evaporating. The problem was one of supplies—food and clothing. Four days after settling in at

Replicated hut, Muhlenberg Brigade, Valley Forge National Historical Park, Valley Forge, Pennsylvania. Washington had his troops build log cabins to get through the winter at Valley Forge because they could be constructed rapidly and inexpensively and were substantially weatherproof.

Valley Forge, Washington wrote that if the quartermaster's corps did not improve its dismal performance, the army was certain to starve, dissolve, or disperse in search of its own provisions.

There was plenty of food in the rich Pennsylvania countryside, but farmers were loath to part with it for the all-but-worthless paper currency—the infamous "Continentals"—with which the army commissaries paid. If that hurdle was cleared, the shortage of wagons and animals and the miserable conditions of the roads made it difficult to haul supplies to Valley Forge. Throughout the winter months the soldiers held out with insufficient food, clothing, and blankets. Only in the spring, when Washington installed a new quartermaster general, did the situation improve.

Eighteenth century armies were composed of professionals, highly trained and disciplined, but the Continental Army was only half a rung above the colonial militias from which it had developed. One general described it as "a mob, not an army." Given the advantage of surprise, as at Trenton, or favorable terrain and logistics, as at Saratoga, it could defeat the enemy. But in pitched battle, opposing British professionals, it was all but hopeless. The great achievement of the months at Valley Forge was the work of a Prussian soldier-of-fortune who went by the name of Baron von Steuben. One of the many out-of-work military men sent to America by Benjamin Franklin, the colonies' envoy in Paris, he impressed Washington and the politicians in Congress to the point of being appointed inspector general of the Continental Army. At first he could not communicate with the troops directly, since he spoke only German and French. But in a matter of weeks he was able to teach the soldiers the skills essential for them to be soldiers.

The army that left Valley Forge in June was still not equipped to take on the Redcoats unaided. But it no longer had to. By then France had concluded a formal alliance with the United States. Ultimately it would dispatch the troops and, above all, the naval forces that were instrumental in persuading the British to recognize American independence.

"Discipline is the soul of an army. It makes small numbers formidable; procures success to the weak, and esteem to all."—George Washington

INDEPENDENCE HALL
Drafting the Declaration of Independence

PHILADELPHIA, PENNSYLVANIA

What we now know as Independence Hall was built to serve as the seat of government for the colony of Pennsylvania. Construction on this building, the Pennsylvania colony's State House, began in 1732 and continued for more than two decades.

The Second Continental Congress convened in the assembly room of this State House in May 1775. It created an army and appointed Col. Washington of Virginia its commander, negotiated with native tribes, and sent diplomatic agents to Europe. The delegates affirmed their loyalty to George III; the colonies' quarrel was with His Majesty's ministers, who were bent on depriving Americans of their rights as freeborn Englishmen.

In January 1776, "Common Sense," a short pamphlet by Thomas Paine, a recent immigrant from England, demonstrated the absurdity of the idea that the king was being misled by his counselors. In May, when the

Independence Hall, Independence National Historical Park, Philadelphia, Pennsylvania. It was first the State House and later called the Hall of Independence. Philadelphia served as American capital from 1777 to 1788, except during British occupation, and as capital of the new republic from 1790 to 1800. It was also the Pennsylvania state capital to 1799.

colonies learned that the British were hiring German mercenaries to put down the rebellion, the Virginia assembly instructed its delegates in Philadelphia to work for independence. On June 7, in the assembly room of the State House, Richard Henry Lee moved that "these United Colonies are, and of right ought to be, Independent States."

Four days later, recognizing that the rupture with Britain was inevitable, Congress appointed a committee to draft a declaration justifying this step: John Adams, Thomas Jefferson, Benjamin Franklin, Roger Sherman, and Robert Livingston.

Jefferson produced a draft that stated the principles of human rights and representative government and enunciated the colonies' grievances. On July 2, Congress passed Lee's motion—in effect, declaring independence. Then it debated various changes in Jefferson's text, which it formally approved on July 4. This became Independence Day, even though, legally speaking, the colonies had already been independent for two days.

Assembly Room, Independence Hall, Independence National Historical Park, Philadelphia, Pennsylvania.

When Congress approved the Declaration on July 4, only the president of Congress, John Hancock, and its secretary, Charles Thomson, affixed their signatures. It was not until August that an engrossed parchment copy was brought to Congress and signed by its current members.

After the War of 1812, with the last survivors of the generation of 1776 rapidly passing from the scene and the country's fiftieth birthday approaching, there was a surge of popular interest in the Declaration. In 1818, Benjamin Owen Tyler published an engraving of the document, featuring carefully executed facsimiles of the signatures on the original. These were felt to add to its authenticity and create a personal link with the patriots who created the document. Other engravings followed—an average of one every two years between 1820 and 1850 and another eight editions before the Civil War. Many American households hung them in the main parlor as a statement of their patriotism. Often other patriotic icons—portraits of presidents and statesmen, the flag, and the Liberty Bell, framed the text.

The State House had served as the seat of the Second Continental Congress from 1775 until its adjournment in 1783 (except for the winter of 1777 to 1778, when Philadelphia was occupied by the British). It was where the Articles of Confederation were adopted in 1781 and the Constitutional Convention met in 1787. It served as the Pennsylvania state capitol building until 1799. Its annexes were home to the Federal Congress and Supreme Court from 1790 until the new U.S. capital of Washington was ready in 1800.

After fifteen years of disuse, plans were announced to raze it. Aghast, the general public raised a subscription and the city of Philadelphia purchased the structure, along with its bell. For Lafayette's visit, in 1824, it was officially renamed the "Hall of Independence."

THE DECLARATION OF INDEPENDENCE
"In Congress, July 4, 1776

The unanimous Declaration of the thirteen united States of America

When in the Course of human events it becomes necessary for one people to dissolve the political bands which have connected them with another and to assume among the powers of the earth, the separate and equal station to which the Laws of Nature and of Nature's God entitle them, a decent respect to the opinions of mankind requires that they should declare the causes which impel them to the separation.

We hold these truths to be self-evident, that all men are created equal, that they are endowed by their Creator with certain unalienable Rights, that among these are Life, Liberty and the pursuit of Happiness. —That to secure these rights, Governments are instituted among Men, deriving their just powers from the consent of the governed,—That whenever any Form of Government becomes destructive of these ends, it is the Right of the People to alter or to abolish it, and to institute new Government, laying its foundation on such principles and organizing its powers in such form, as to them shall seem most likely to effect their Safety and Happiness..."

BRITISH NORTH AMERICA

ATLANTIC OCEAN

——— U.S. borders today

▨ Settled areas in 1790

THE THIRTEEN UNITED STATES & BEYOND (1790)

The thirteen colonies formed what the Declaration of Independence called "the united States of America." By 1790, all thirteen colonies were admitted.

ORIGINAL THIRTEEN COLONIES Constitution, June 14, 1777	
State or Commonwealth	**Date Ratified the Constitution**
Delaware	December 7, 1787
Pennsylvania	December 12, 1787
New Jersey	December 18, 1787
Georgia	January 2, 1788
Connecticut	January 9, 1788
Massachusetts	February 6, 1788
Maryland	April 28, 1788
South Carolina	May 23, 1788
New Hampshire	June 21, 1788
Virginia	June 25, 1788
New York	July 26, 1788
North Carolina	November 21, 1789
Rhode Island	May 29, 1790

The thirteen original colonies extended from New Hampshire in the northeast down to Georgia in the South. Vermont and Maine, sometimes considered part of New England, were not yet part of the United States. New York state had made claims on the lands east, today's Vermont, and England still had a bite out of today's Maine, which had once been considered an extension of the Massachusetts Bay Colony. At the time of the Declaration of Independence, the cities of Boston, Philadelphia, New York, Charleston, Savannah, Raleigh, Baltimore, Providence, and Richmond had already been established.

In the Northwest Territory by 1790, Detroit had existed as a major fur-trading center on the Great Lakes for nearly a century. Chicago, however, had not yet been founded. New Orleans was well-established, under French and Spanish rule, and thriving in what later became the Louisiana Territory.

LIBERTY BELL

Let Freedom Ring

"Yes there's a lady that stands in a harbor for what we believe. And there's a bell that still echoes the price that it cost to be free."—Aaron Tippen, "Where the Stars and Stripes and Eagles Fly"

INDEPENDENCE HALL AND GREEN, PHILADELPHIA, PENNSYLVANIA

What we know today as the Liberty Bell was rung in July 1776 to announce the Declaration of Independence. Independence Hall, the State House of the colony of Pennsylvania, had a bell hung in its steeple that could not be heard all over Philadelphia, so a larger one was ordered from England. First hung in 1753 to celebrate the fiftieth anniversary of the colony of Pennsylvania's charter, the bell, today's Liberty Bell, bears an inscription found in the book of Leviticus 25.10, which begins, "And ye shall hallow the fiftieth year," and continues, "Proclaim liberty throughout all the land unto all the inhabitants thereof." The ill-starred bell cracked the first time it was rung. Two local craftsmen melted it down and recast it; this time the tone was too dull. They tried again; the tone still disappointed some. Another bell was ordered from England. When it arrived, the Assembly decided it sounded no better than the one already hanging in the steeple and found another use for the newcomer.

Liberty Bell, Independence National Historical Park, Philadelphia, Pennsylvania.

The State House bell tolled to celebrate significant occasions, including the coronation of George III in 1763, the passage and later repeal of the Stamp Act, the convening of the First Continental Congress in nearby Carpenters' Hall in 1774, and the battles of Lexington and Concord in 1775. It was probably rung on July 8, 1776, to summon the townspeople to the first public reading of the Declaration of Independence.

The close link between the Declaration and the State House bell was forged in 1847, in one of George Lippard's didactic "legends." Lippard wrote about the elderly bellman who, on July 4, 1776, is waiting for word that the Continental Congress has declared independence—until, finally, his grandson calls up to him, "Ring!" The old man, feeling young again, rings vigorously, and "the crowds in the street burst forth in one long shout." Lippard knew it hadn't happened that way; he wanted to convey a deeper message.

For Lippard was also a prominent abolitionist. The bell's association with the antislavery movement, based on its inscription, with the emphasis on "*all* the inhabitants thereof," dates from 1837, when it appeared as the frontispiece to a publication of the New York Anti-Slavery Society. Two years later, William Lloyd Garrison's *The Liberator* reprinted a poem entitled "The Liberty Bell"—the first known use of that name for the bell in what was by that time known as Independence Hall.

The bell was removed from the top of the steeple in 1828, when a new bell was installed, and placed in a lower room. There it continued to be rung on major occasions, including Washington's birthday. A hairline crack appeared at some time between 1817 and 1846. No conclusive evidence points to a particular date, although around 1876 it was fashionable to associate the crack with significant occasions, such as Lafayette's visit or Chief Justice John Marshall's funeral (1835). What is documented is that an attempt was made to repair the bell by filing the hairline crack (thus producing the familiar half-inch slit 24 inches long). The repair was successful and the bell pealed acceptably on Monday, February 23, 1846, in honor of Washington's birthday. But at the last stroke it cracked again, all the way to the crown—this time beyond repair.

In 1911, an 86-year-old Pennsylvanian named Rauch reported that in 1835 the superintendent of the bell tower had tied a rope to the clapper and invited a passing group of boys, of whom he was one, to ring it in honor of Washington's birthday. After about a dozen strokes they heard a change in the tone. Discovering a crack about a foot long, the keeper sent the boys packing. Many have dismissed this story as an old man's fantasy, especially since the bell was rung for another eleven years. But the crack reported in Rauch's account is only about half as long as that repaired a decade later—suggesting that Philadelphians continued to ring the bell, unaware of the flaw, for a number of years. Bell makers say that swinging the clapper directly can indeed cause a bell to crack.

BETSY ROSS HOUSE

The American Flag: From Sons of Liberty Stripes to Fifty Stars

PHILADELPHIA, PENNSYLVANIA

The American colonies' quarrel with King George III of England was reflected in the Grand Union flag raised by Washington outside Boston on New Year's Day 1776: thirteen stripes, representing the United Colonies, and the Union Jack, symbolizing their bond with Great Britain, in the canton.

The dissolution of the tie with Britain made the Grand Union flag unsuitable. But almost a year passed before the Congressional journal for June 14, 1777, reported: "Resolved, That the flag of the United States be made of thirteen stripes, alternate red and white; that the union be thirteen stars, white in a blue field, representing a new Constellation." As far as can be demonstrated from contemporary sources, this flag was first flown over Fort Schuyler (present-day Rome, New York), in August 1777. Who originated the familiar stars and stripes design?

Addressing the Historical Society of Pennsylvania in 1870, William Canby presented a story circulating in his family: that to his grandmother, Elizabeth Claypoole—Betsy Ross, as she was in 1776—"belongs the honor of having made with her own hands the first flag." Canby recounted how a secret committee of the Continental Congress, including General Washington and Col. George Ross, her late husband's uncle, called on her in her upholstery shop with a sketch of a flag and asked if she could sew it. According to Canby, his grandmother, who had no experience in flag making, found fault with the design—notably that the stars were six- rather than five-pointed—and the committee accepted her modifications. She sewed the flag, which was approved by Congress the next day. Canby does not state when this meeting took place; an affidavit sworn to by his nonagenarian aunt, Rachel Fletcher, dates it to June 1776.

THE AMERICAN FLAG

Sons of Liberty Flag   *Thirteen Colonies Flag*   *Flag with Fifty Stars*

The British Union Jack was the first flag flown in the colonies. In the 1770s American patriots created the Sons of Liberty flag, which had 13 red and white stripes to represent the 13 colonies. The Continental Colors or Grand Union flag combined the 13 stripes with the Union Jack in the upper left corner in 1775. The first Stars and Stripes, a flag with 13 red and white stripes and a circle of 13 white stars on a blue field in the upper left corner reportedly resembles that sewn by Betsy Ross (someone else may have devised the design). The Continental Congress approved the stars and stripes design on June 14, 1777. Other versions of this 13-13 flag arrange the constellation of stars differently.

Francis Scott Key's "Star-Spangled Banner," a flag of 1814 that flew over Fort McHenry, had 15 stars and stripes. A 1794 act of Congress adopted the 15-15 flag after Vermont joined the Union in 1791 and Kentucky in 1792.

The number of stripes was fixed at 13 by 1818, but the star arrangement varied. Just before the Civil War, the flag had 34 stars for 34 states; none were removed when the South seceded. In 1912, a presidential order fixed the position of the flag's then 48 stars for America's 48 states. The 49th star for Alaska was added on July 4, 1959, and the 50th for Hawaii on July 4, 1960 to create our familiar Stars and Stripes.

Harper's Monthly gave the story national play in July 1873. During the next decade it became standard fare in schoolbooks. *Birth of Our Nation's Flag*, a depiction of the meeting by painter Casper Weisgerber, was exhibited at the 1893 World Columbian Exposition in Chicago. After that, "Betsy Ross designed the flag" was a firmly ensconced item of Americana.

Betsy Ross certainly made flags in later years. But the only person who ever publicly asserted parenthood of the American flag was Francis Hopkinson, a New Jersey delegate to the Continental Congress. In 1780 he submitted a claim that he had designed "the flag of the United States of America" and various other devices, including the Great Seal of the United States, and requested, by way of remuneration, "a Quarter Cask of the public wine." Hopkinson's political enemies used various stratagems to parry his claim; he never did get the wine. But none of these men, who must have been privy to the activities of Congress during 1776–1777, ever objected that Hopkinson had not designed the flag.

Some points where the Canby-Fletcher account might be challenged turn out to be plausible. Although Washington left Philadelphia in June 1775, when appointed commander-in-chief, he was in town for consultations with Congress in late May and early June 1776, when his meeting with Betsy Ross is supposed to have taken place. Other details do not jibe. The 1777 Congressional resolution did not specify five-pointed stars; many early banners had seven- or eight-pointed stars. That Washington was no longer a member of Congress in 1776 may not be relevant, since he was commander-in-chief and is known to have been interested in a flag for his troops. But George Ross, supposed to have been a member of the secret committee, was not a delegate to Congress in May–July 1776. The incautious might be tripped up, though, because Ross did sign the Declaration of Independence.

What about the recollections of the aged Betsy Ross and her even older daughter? Or Thomas Jefferson's claim that he had a vivid recollection of a July 4, 1776, signing ceremony that never took place?

Texts turn into icons. Icons spawn myths. And myths, if we treat them with due skepticism and due reverence, may express a higher truth. Asked his opinion of the Betsy Ross legend, Woodrow Wilson—a trained historian before entering politics—replied, "would that it were true!"

Betsy Ross House, Philadelphia, Pennsylvania. Betsy Ross was a seamstress reportedly given the task of sewing the first flag of the new Thirteen American Colonies.

FORT MCHENRY

War of 1812 & "The Star-Spangled Banner"

"We, Sir, are ready at Fort McHenry to defend Baltimore against invading by the enemy. This is to say, we are ready except that we have no suitable ensign to display over the Star Fort, and it is my desire to have a flag so large that the British will have no difficulty in seeing it from a distance."—from a letter of Maj. George Armistead, commanding officer of Fort McHenry

BALTIMORE, MARYLAND

The War of 1812 was a military and political stalemate ended by a treaty that restored the status quo ante, except for the lives of hundreds of soldiers and civilians. Aside from accelerating the dispossession of the Creek Nation in what became Alabama and Mississippi, it had only two lasting effects: Andrew Jackson's elevation to the presidency, 14 years after his victory at the Battle of New Orleans; and the composition of what eventually became the national anthem.

When war broke out between Revolutionary France and Britain in the 1790s and Congress upgraded the defenses along the Atlantic seacoast, the earthwork fort guarding Baltimore harbor was rebuilt in stone and named for James McHenry, Revolutionary War soldier, Maryland delegate to the Constitutional Convention, and secretary of war under Washington and Adams.

Fort McHenry cannons overlooking Baltimore Harbor, Baltimore, Maryland.

Fort McHenry, Baltimore, Maryland.

In the spring of 1812, pent-up anti-British feeling, fanned by Britain's high-handed treatment of U.S. merchant shipping, ignited an American declaration of war. As long as Napoleon pinned down most British forces, the United States had slightly the better of the rather desultory conflict, especially on the Great Lakes and at sea. But after Bonaparte was banished to Elba, in early 1814, the British sent veterans of the European conflict to teach the Americans a lesson. They occupied parts of Maine and Massachusetts and prepared to assault other vulnerable coastal towns, including Washington and nearby Baltimore. The American defense of Washington was a fiasco; on August 24, British troops occupied the town almost without opposition. They set fire to the Capitol, the Executive Mansion, and other public and private buildings (provident or patriotic cloudbursts saved them from total destruction) before heading north for Baltimore.

On September 12, the British ground assault stalled when its commander, Maj. Gen. Robert Ross, was fatally wounded by a sharpshooter. The naval flotilla stood out of range of Fort McHenry's guns and dispatched five mortar boats—floating platforms whose cannons were designed to launch "bombs" (hollow spheres filled with a fused explosive charge, rather than the more traditional solid cannonballs) and Congreve rockets—to reduce the fort.

Flying over Fort McHenry was a 30x42-foot flag, commissioned the year before. Each of its fifteen stars measured 2 feet across; each of its fifteen stripes was 2 feet wide.

Francis Scott Key, a 35-year-old Georgetown attorney who had been rowed out to the British flagship several days earlier to negotiate the release of an elderly prisoner, was detained there before and during the bombardment. Although he was a Federalist and no supporter of the war, Key's patriotic sentiments were aroused by the British officers' hatred for everything American and the unremitting bombardment of the fort, which continued through the night of September 12–13. When morning revealed the fort intact, with the huge banner flying above it, he quickly penned four stanzas on the back of a letter he found in his pocket. He fit the words to a patriotic song entitled "Adams and Liberty," which in turn was sung to the tune of the anthem of a London gentleman's club, "To Anacreon in Heaven." (The tune seems to have had no single composer, though John Stafford Smith, the composer of "God Save the King" ["My Country 'Tis of Thee"], would have been prominent among those involved.) Friends had it printed on handbills under the heading, "The Defence of Fort McHenry." A few weeks later, when it appeared in a newspaper, it was entitled "The Star-Spangled Banner."

During the Civil War, the flag was a prominent symbol of loyalty, so Union army bands played the song frequently. Later, John Philip Sousa would close his concerts with a spirited rendition. In 1916, making a decades-old custom official, President Woodrow Wilson ordered it played at all military ceremonies. "The Star-Spangled Banner" made its baseball debut at the 1918 World Series. Finally, in 1931, Congress officially adopted it as the national anthem.

> *"O say, does that star-spangled banner yet wave*
> *O'er the land of the free and the home of the brave?"*
> —Francis Scott Key, 1814

THE COLLEGE OF WILLIAM & MARY

Education, Freeing the American Mind

"[B]y going to the College [William and Mary] I shall get a more universal Acquaintance, which may hereafter be serviceable to me; and I suppose I can pursue my Studies in the Greek and Latin as well there as here, and likewise learn something of the Mathematics."—Thomas Jefferson, 1760

WILLIAMSBURG, VIRGINIA

For the Puritan founders of New England, the Bible was the source of all truth, accessible to every member of the community. To achieve this end, literacy was essential, and they drew from among themselves a learned clergy who focused on the Bible, other texts, and theology. Their divines were expected to be fluent in Hebrew, Greek, and Latin. To satisfy this need, the General Court of the Massachusetts Bay Colony established a college to train clergymen in 1636. Three years later, the Court renamed the school Harvard College, in recognition of a bequest by John Harvard of Charlestown. Despite this legacy, the college survived only because the colonists—poor farmers and rich merchants alike—continued to support it with their taxes and contributions.

Although Harvard College, founded in 1636, was the first college in English America, the Spanish had already established several universities in their colonies. The College of William and Mary is the second oldest college in English America.

Wren Building, The College of William and Mary, Williamsburg, Virginia.

The College of William & Mary, Williamsburg, Virginia.

The farther south one traveled in the colonies, the less emphasis was placed on education. Anglicanism did not mandate an educated laity, and clergymen could be imported from the mother country. The gentry on their country plantations employed tutors for their children and had no interest in paying taxes to help educate the middle and lower classes in the towns.

For most of the 17th century, those few who wanted a higher education were sent back to Oxford or Cambridge to acquire it.

It was only in 1691 that the colonial assembly dispatched the Rev. James Blair, the senior Anglican cleric in Virginia, to London to obtain a charter for a collegiate school. In February 1693, William III and Mary II granted a charter for "a perpetual College of Divinity, Philosophy, Languages, and other Arts and Sciences, consisting of one President, six Masters or Professors, and a hundred Scholars more or less." Of equal importance to the charter was the royal endowment that came with it.

Construction of the first building for the new collegiate school in Williamsburg (at the time still known as Middle Plantation) began in 1695. Completed by 1699, it combined the functions of student dormitory, lecture hall, library, and faculty common room and living quarters. Originally known simply as "the College," in the 20th century it was renamed the Wren Building, in recognition of an 18th century tradition that it was based on a design by the famous architect Sir Christopher Wren. It is the oldest academic structure in the United States, antedating Massachusetts Hall at Harvard and Connecticut Hall at Yale by more than 20 and 50 years, respectively. The claim that the Wren Building is the oldest continuously used academic building in the country is inaccurate, however, since the building was destroyed by fire three times (1705, 1859, and 1862) and William and Mary itself suspended operations and held no classes between the Civil War and 1888.

Throughout the 18th century and the first quarter of the 19th, until the founding of the University of Virginia, William and Mary was the premier institution of higher learning in the southern colonies. Its most famous alumnus—then or since—was Thomas Jefferson. But the demand for advanced education continued to expand in New England and the Middle Colonies. Before the Revolutionary War, seven more colleges were established: Yale in 1701; Princeton, 1743 (officially the College of New Jersey until 1896); the University of Pennsylvania, 1749; King's College (now Columbia), 1754; Brown, 1764; Queen's College (now Rutgers), 1766 (first classes 1771); and Dartmouth, 1769.

LAND-GRANT COLLEGES

Land-grant colleges date from 1862 and the First Morrill Act. Today, over 105 land-grant colleges and universities compete with private universities for students and make higher education more accessible to rich and poor.

The Act provides support for colleges of agriculture and mechanical arts in each state. Subsequent acts provided for land-grant Native American tribal colleges and colleges in Guam, Puerto Rico, and the Virgin Islands.

MOUNT VERNON

George Washington, Gentleman Farmer

"I can truly say that I had rather be at home at Mount Vernon with a friend or two about me, than to be attended at the seat of the government by the officers of State and the representatives of every power in Europe."
—George Washington

MOUNT VERNON, VIRGINIA

Men with a far better education and broader experience—Franklin, Jefferson, Madison, Hamilton, Jay, and others—created the theoretical basis and political structure of the new country. But it was George Washington, trained in the very practical trade of surveying, who took the blueprint contained in the founding documents, especially the Constitution, and erected an edifice of government that has endured for more than two centuries. As president, knowing that his every step set an example that would guide if not bind his successors, he moved slowly and cautiously. The cabinet was his invention; so, too, the decision to leave the vice president as a figurehead rather than make him a deputy president or prime minister. His decision to retire after two terms—an absolute break with the last vestiges of monarchy and a precedent whose contribution to a stable democratic system cannot be overestimated, though we take it for granted today—established a principle so important that it was ultimately enshrined in the Constitution itself.

Already in his lifetime he was acclaimed "the father of his country." More than two generations after his death, the fresco on the inside of the Capitol dome would depict nothing less than the "Apotheosis of George Washington." That was the exalted status he had achieved in the American collective memory, though clearly Washington the man would have rejected this spurious divinity just as he refused a royal crown.

Washington was not given to humility. Though he did not seek the positions of high responsibility thrust upon him—commander-in-chief of the Continental Army and president—he accepted them as a duty, conscious that, although there might be other worthy candidates, he was no less qualified than any of them. What was special about him—the incredible stroke of fortune that made possible the birth and long-term survival of the United States—was the extent to which he was a modern embodiment of the Roman general Cincinnatus, who, when the war was won, returned to plowing his field behind his oxen. The American people's appreciation of his

The Mansion, George Washington's Mount Vernon Estate & Gardens, Mount Vernon, Virginia.

demonstration of this supreme republican virtue is indicated by the fact that the eighth and last (in historical sequence) of the paintings in the Capitol Rotunda is of Washington resigning his commission at the end of the Revolutionary War.

When he did so, it was to return to Mount Vernon, the estate he had inherited from his half-brother and more than tripled in size. There, he wrote to a friend, he planned to "spend the remainder of [his] days in cul-

tivating the affections of good men and in the practice of domestic Virtues." Although the young republic called him back to its service—and his sense of duty compelled him to respond—his fondest wish remained, as before, to return to the life of the gentleman farmer.

Many places in America boast "George Washington slept here." But only Mount Vernon was home—that, and the country he fathered. His tomb bears the inscription "General Washington"; his wife Martha's, the monarchical epithet "consort." But these are the work of other hands. His own perspective—and the reason he was and remains "first in the hearts of his countrymen" is summarized in the phrase by which he identified himself in his will: "George Washington, of Mount Vernon, a citizen of the United States."

Outbuildings, or dependencies, George Washington's Mount Vernon Estate and Gardens, Mount Vernon, Virginia.

GEORGE WASHINGTON'S 1789 THANKSGIVING PROCLAMATION

"Whereas it is the duty of all nations to acknowledge the providence of Almighty God, to obey His will, to be grateful for His benefits, and humbly to implore His protection and favor; and Whereas both Houses of Congress have, by their joint committee, requested me "to recommend to the people of the United States a day of public thanksgiving and prayer, to be observed by acknowledging with grateful hearts the many and signal favors of Almighty God, especially by affording them an opportunity peaceably to establish a form of government for their safety and happiness:

Now, therefore, I do recommend and assign Thursday, the 26th day of November next, to be devoted by the people of these States to the service of that great and glorious Being who is the beneficent author of all the good that was, that is, or that will be; that we may then all unite in rendering unto Him our sincere and humble thanks for His kind care and protection of the people of this country previous to their becoming a nation; for the signal and manifold mercies and the favorable interpositions of His providence in the course and conclusion of the late war; for the great degree of tranquility, union, and plenty which we have since enjoyed; for the peaceable and rational manner in which we have been enable to establish constitutions of government for our safety and happiness, and particularly the national one now lately instituted; for the civil and religious liberty with which we are blessed, and the means we have of acquiring and diffusing useful knowledge; and, in general, for all the great and various favors which He has been pleased to confer upon us.

And also that we may then unite in most humbly offering our prayers and supplications to the great Lord and Ruler of Nations and beseech Him to pardon our national and other transgressions; to enable us all, whether in public or private stations, to perform our several and relative duties properly and punctually; to render our National Government a blessing to all the people by constantly being a Government of wise, just, and constitutional laws, discreetly and faithfully executed and obeyed; to protect and guide all sovereigns and nations (especially such as have shown kindness to us), and to bless them with good governments, peace, and concord; to promote the knowledge and practice of true religion and virtue, and the increase of science among them and us; and, generally to grant unto all mankind such a degree of temporal prosperity as He alone knows to be best.

Given under my hand, at the city of New York, the 3d dy of October, A.D. 1789.   (signed) G. Washington"

MONTICELLO

Thomas Jefferson, the Pursuit of Happiness

"No occupation is so delightful to me as the culture of earth, and no culture comparable to that of the garden. But though an old man I am but a young gardener."—Thomas Jefferson to Charles Willson Peale, 1811

CHARLOTTESVILLE, VIRGINIA

When Peter Jefferson, Thomas's father, came to Goochland (later Albemarle) County in the early 1730s, it was the western frontier of Virginia. Its open horizons beckoned to the younger sons and new arrivals who were carving out their own plantations there.

Peter himself was a well-known surveyor and mapmaker. Those were important skills in a society where land was wealth and broad acres could be obtained through connections with the governor and his council. Among Peter Jefferson's neighbors and associates was Dr. Thomas Walker (young Thomas's guardian after Peter's death in 1757), the physician-explorer who discovered Cumberland Gap during his four-month trek to central Kentucky in 1750. Walker and his associates even considered an expedition to explore the Missouri River and find a route to the Pacific. The outbreak of the French and Indian War in 1754 forced them to cancel the plan.

The Lewis and Clark expedition was Jefferson's fourth attempt to learn more about western North America. In 1783, Revolutionary War hero George Rogers Clark declined his request to lead a trans-Mississippi expedition. In 1787, while serving as American minister in Paris, Jefferson was among the sponsors of a plan to send John Ledyard across Russia and thence to the Pacific coast; this came to naught when Ledyard was expelled

Monticello and west lawn, Monticello, Charlottesville, Virginia. In Thomas Jefferson and other founding fathers we find the intellectual roots of our democracy, although Jefferson, like many other 18th century men, owned slaves. His will specified that they be freed after he died. Courtesy of Monticello/Thomas Jefferson Foundation, Inc.

Vegetable garden and pavillion, Monticello, Charlottesville, Virginia. The pavillion was one of Jefferson's favorite places to sit and read. Courtesy of Monticello/Thomas Jefferson Foundation, Inc.

from Russia. In 1793, Jefferson and fellow members of the American Philosophical Society hired French botanist André Michaux to explore the Missouri River and Pacific Northwest. This venture crashed when Michaux turned out to be a French secret agent.

In arranging the Louisiana Purchase and dispatching Meriwether Lewis and William Clark (both of them originally from Albemarle County), President Jefferson was faithful to his Albemarle antecedents. In his first inaugural address (1801) he spoke of "a rising nation, spread over a wide and fruitful land, advancing rapidly to destinies beyond the reach of mortal eye." Almost two years later, in a secret message to Congress, he noted that the Indian tribes were becoming less willing to sell land to whites. To acquire the territory that the rapid expansion of the country's population required, he proposed seducing them with manufactured goods to increase their domestic comfort and replace their extensive land use and hunting-based economy with intensive agriculture, thereby bringing them to "agriculture, manufactures, and civilization."

This trinity was epitomized at Monticello (Italian for "hillock"; as the good people of Albemarle County will tell you, it is pronounced *montichello*), Jefferson's 5,000-acre plantation near Charlottesville. The four farms attached to the estate raised various crops and livestock—some for home consumption, most for sale. The manor house was surrounded by kitchen gardens and various outbuildings and workshops where skilled craftsmen produced the basic requirements of the plantation—cheeses and hams, bricks, nails, barrels, cloth, and simple furniture.

That manor house—portrayed on the reverse of the nickel—was designed by Jefferson himself, based on the ideas of the leading architects of the age. Construction began in 1769 and was just about complete when Jefferson departed for Paris in 1784. It was remodeled and enlarged between 1796 and 1809. Jefferson continued to remodel the house throughout his life.

From its contents, visitors could not tell that Monticello was in upcountry America rather than in France or Italy. Most notable was Jefferson's private library. Throughout his life Jefferson was an inveterate book collector; his chief delight during his years in Paris was scouring the bookstores for volumes about America and natural science.

"Enlighten the people generally, and tyranny and oppressions of body and mind will vanish like evil spirits at the dawn of day."—Thomas Jefferson to P. S. Dupont de Nemours, 1816

OLD SLAVE MART

Where Liberty Was Sold to the Highest Bidder

"The right to freedom being the gift of God, it is not in the power of man to alienate this gift and voluntarily become a slave."—Samuel Adams

CHARLESTON, SOUTH CAROLINA

On the eve of the Civil War, white Southerners (as well as a few free blacks and Native Americans) owned nearly 4 million African slaves—an asset roughly equal in value to all the farmland and farm buildings in the South. In the seven cotton states, slaves made up nearly half the population and produced 31% of the whites' income.

Indentured servants (including the first blacks in Jamestown, in 1619) were the original machinery of colonial times. By 1776, though, they had been almost totally replaced by African slaves—about 539,000, more than 90% of them in the southern colonies (Maryland south to Georgia). Starting with the Republic of Vermont in 1777, northern jurisdictions gradually abolished slavery. (Vermont became the 14th state in 1791.) After all, they

Old Slave Mart, Charleston, South Carolina. The prosperity of the Old South was built on the unwilling backs of African slaves, who received food, shelter, and often abuse in return for their toil, tears, and lost liberty. Many disobedient slaves were whipped and many escaped slaves were hung.

had just subscribed themselves to the proposition that "all men are created equal." And although blacks were universally acknowledged to be inferior, morally and mentally, their humanity was not denied.

The emancipation process never took hold in the South. One reason was its much larger black population—whites outnumbered blacks by less than two to one (by 1860 they were a minority in South Carolina and Mississippi)—and the social and economic dislocation that even gradual emancipation would have entailed. Another was the deepening sense that the South's "peculiar institution" (peculiar in the sense of distinctive) was the crux of its culture and identity. Slavery was the dominant issue of American politics from 1830 to 1865 because the South was fighting to defend its way of life against the more populous North and could not imagine itself without slavery. It rejected even gradual compensated emancipation with repatriation of the freedmen and freedwomen to Africa.

In the decades before the Civil War, one state after another restricted owners' previously uncontested right to free their slaves. In part this was benevolent social legislation that prevented cynical masters from freeing old or disabled slaves to starve or be supported by the taxpayers. But it was also a reaction to the growing abolitionist sentiment in the North. Many states even made it illegal to teach slaves to read and write.

Slave owners could do just about anything to their slaves, except perhaps kill them in cold blood. They resorted to the lash because they had no other effective means of coercion, on the one hand, and because of the prevalent view that blacks were like children and should be punished the same way when they disobeyed. There was legislation against excessive abuse—not out of sympathy for slaves, but because of fears that it might provoke insurrection. These laws were largely a dead letter, though, because slaves and wives could not testify in court against male heads of household, and other slave owners were unlikely to do so. On the other hand, the courts treated slaves harshly; in many states, the law stipulated much more severe penalties for their crimes than for the same action by a free white.

The domestic slave trade thrived and slave markets were found in every Southern town. The constant drain of slaves from the upper South to the Cotton Belt indicates the economic voltage of slavery. Insubordinate slaves were continually threatened that they would be "sold down the river"; bankruptcy or the sale of an estate could work the same fate for larger groups. The salience of the process, which callously disrupted black family life, is reflected not just in Harriet Beecher Stowe's abolitionist novel, *Uncle Tom's Cabin* (1852), but also in the songs of Stephen Foster—"my Old Kentucky home *far away*," "still longing for the old plantation." A contemporary observer calculated that about 2% of all slaves were sold each year. New Orleans had the largest slave market, followed by Richmond, Natchez, and Charleston.

As practiced in the antebellum South, slavery was more profitable than free labor, offering an average return of about 10%. Plantation families were not its only beneficiaries. So were the owners of textile mills in England and New England, their employees (notorious anti-abolitionists in the 1830s and 1840s), and everyone who wore inexpensive cotton clothing. Massachusetts Sen. Charles Sumner said the system was "an unholy union between the lords of the lash and the lords of the loom," all of them growing rich on the sweat and tears of black slaves.

> **WEEKLY RATIONS**
> According to archaeologists, plantation records, and diaries, an average weekly food ration for an adult slave was about 1 peck (8 quarts) cornmeal, 1 pound salt beef or pork, and a little molasses or salt fish. That's around 2,000 calories a day—not enough to sustain hard labor.
>
> Archeologists have found bone fragments in sub-floor pits of slave cabins in Virginia that suggest that slaves hunted and fished to supplement their meager rations. At some plantations, like Mount Vernon, slaves were permitted to maintain their own gardens.

"A house divided against itself cannot stand. I believe this government cannot endure permanently half slave and half free."—Abraham Lincoln, 1858

PLANTATIONS
Idyll of the Southern Aristocracy

"The haughty and imperious part of a man develops rapidly on one of these lonely sugar plantations, where the owner rarely meets with anyone except his slaves and minions."—President Rutherford B. Hayes (1822–1893)

THE OLD SOUTH

Southern plantations relied on slave labor to grow cotton, tobacco (in Virginia and North Carolina), rice (in South Carolina), and sugar (in Louisiana), but it was cotton that drove the economy. In the 18th century, cotton was grown in South Carolina and Georgia. Cotton cultivation spread into the Piedmont districts of the Carolinas and Georgia, displacing the yeoman farmers. Later the native tribes were forced out of Georgia, Alabama, and Mississippi, and planters cleared the empty land for cotton.

Mansion, Oak Alley Plantation, Vacherie, Louisiana. A wealthy French Creole sugar planter from New Orleans built Oak Alley Plantation, called the grande dame of the Great River Road, in 1839 on the Mississippi River between New Orleans and Baton Rouge, Louisiana.

Giant 300-year-old oak trees create a canopy one-fourth mile long on Oak Alley Plantation in Vacherie, Louisiana.

Slaveholders were actually in the minority in the antebellum South. In 1860, fewer than 25% of white Southern households owned slaves and less than 1% of slave owners held more than 100. The average number of slaves in a single household was around ten. A "planter" had to own at least 20 slaves; by this definition, only 3% of white Southern males were planters in 1860. This small minority constituted the unchallenged economic, political, and social elite. The refined plantation society of the Tidewater, whose roots went back several generations, with its mansions and strong family ties, was very different from the parvenu cotton frontier, where the "big house" was often far from elegant and some planters might not want to flaunt their ancestry. It was an aristocracy of wealth, not birth, however, and any white man could aspire to join their ranks.

The majority of Southern whites were yeoman farmers who owned few or no slaves and worked their own farms with the help of their families. They were not poor, but the slave economy left them at an economic disadvantage. They supported slavery because of their ingrained racism and fears of what emancipation might bring. At the bottom of the heap, the poor whites heartily resented the planters, but liked blacks even less. By keeping blacks down, lower-class whites ensured that they would not occupy the bottom rung of the social ladder themselves.

The storied plantation life of leisure is a myth. A Southern belle may have led a carefree life, with frequent parties and balls, as she cast about for her dream cavalier. Once married, however, she assumed the immense responsibilities of managing the plantation, except for those associated with raising and selling the staple crop, which kept her husband occupied full time. The mistress of the plantation oversaw the care and feeding of her family and of the slaves. Like the lady of a medieval castle, she always kept the keys to the pantry and other domestic storehouses on her person. The drudgery of laundry, cooking, and cleaning was handled by slaves, of course, but supervising them was a constant chore.

Slaves resisted their owners in many ways—vandalizing or stealing their property, slacking off in the fields, running away. They dissembled their true feelings, since these were not acceptable to their masters. But the deceit could never be totally hidden and whites castigated blacks as shiftless and untrustworthy. Violent resist-

Slave Street, Boone Hall Plantation, Mount Pleasant, South Carolina. Boone Hall Plantation was part of a series of land grants from South Carolina's Lords Proprietors to Major John Boone, the earliest grant dating from 1681. The cotton plantation, spread over thousands of acres, became a giant of the Low Country's plantation culture. Slave quarters on many other plantations were often less sturdily built and few dwellings have survived from the mid-19th century.

SLAVE QUARTERS

Generally, nine or more slaves, often from different families, shared a small cabin perhaps no larger than 10x12 feet, usually with a dirt floor. Cabins were constructed with logs and mud, tabby (oyster shells, lime, and cement), adobe, or, less often, brick. Few remain standing today. Slave quarters close to the main house were more attractive and built of sturdier materials to prevent danger to the plantation's mansion through fire. Cabins were simply furnished and more than one person shared a bunk. Many individuals dug pits in the ground inside the cabin to hide personal belongings or store food.

ance was rare, peaking in Denmark Vesey's conspiracy in South Carolina (1822) and Nat Turner's rebellion in Virginia (1831), in which more than fifty whites were killed. Reacting to the latter, a special Virginia convention on slavery, held the next winter, defeated various emancipation proposals and approved tighter controls over slaves, including restrictions on their freedom of movement and assembly, education, and manumission.

Few Northerners thought that blacks were the equals of whites. But Southern whites were utterly enslaved to a deep-seated conviction in the primordial inferiority of blacks. Black slavery, they held, was not founded on "the pride, the power, and the avarice of man" (Frederick Douglass) but was an essential part of the divine plan or natural order. For John C. Calhoun, slavery was "the most safe and stable basis for free institutions in the world." His political heirs saw no contradiction between proclaiming that the Confederacy was waging a war for freedom and human rights and the harsh repression on which their social order was based. Howell Cobb of Georgia, one of the largest slave owners in the South, epitomized their creed in a single line: "If the black will make a good soldier, our entire theory of slavery is wrong."

COTTON FIELDS

White Gold, the Pick & the Price

"I wish I was in the land of cotton,
Old times there are not forgotten,
Look away! Look away! Look away! Dixie Land.
In Dixie Land where I was born in
Early on one frosty morning"'
—from Daniel Decatur Emmett's song "Dixie"

THE OLD SOUTH & NEW COTTON BELT

Cotton is king!" "proclaimed Sen. James Hammond of South Carolina in 1858, meaning that the North could never impose its will on the South militarily, because the whole world was economically dependent on cotton. In 1860, King Cotton ruled the South, which produced two-thirds of the world supply. Cotton ruled the West and Midwest, which fed the South to the tune of $30 million a year. Cotton ruled the Northeast, whose textile mills turned out $100 million worth of cloth a year, while its factories sold the South more than $150 million worth of manufactured goods.

Cotton was grown on the South Carolina and Georgia coast in the 18th century, but it was only marginally profitable because of the immense amount of hand labor required to deseed it. This changed in 1793, when Eli

Cotton Fields, The Cotton Trail, Cheraw, South Carolina.

Society Hill Library, Society Hill, South Carolina. The Society Hill Library was organized in 1822 using $240 donated from each of the founding fathers. It was one of the reasons that Society Hill became the cultural center of the Pee Dee region.

The Cotton Belt, once confined to the Old South, today extends from North Carolina to South Carolina, Georgia, Alabama, Mississippi, Louisiana, and into parts of Tennessee, Kentucky, Arkansas, Texas, Oklahoma, Virginia, California, and Florida.

Whitney invented the cotton gin, which was eight to ten times faster than hand culling at separating the seeds from the fiber. In 1804 the cotton crop was eight times as large as it had been a decade earlier; production increased another fiftyfold by 1860. The mechanization of textile mills with the Industrial Revolution helped cotton become more important than flax and wool textiles in the international market.

But like any despotic monarch, King Cotton could not abide competition. The South was underdeveloped because nothing could vie with plantation agriculture. It was underdeveloped because immigrants preferred to settle in the North, where black slaves would not price them out of the labor market. It remained overwhelmingly rural, because the plantation economy did not need a large urban merchant and artisan class. Except for New Orleans, no city in the Confederacy had ranked among the 20 largest cities in the United States in 1860.

MILL TOWNS
Northern Factories & Textile Mills

LOWELL, MASSACHUSETTS

In 1790, nine of ten Americans lived on farms; most of their utensils and implements were imported, home-made, or produced in small workshops. The economic and political history of the United States from then until the Civil War can be summarized in one word: cotton. It was cotton that sustained slavery, primed the Industrial Revolution that brought prosperity and victory to the North, and catalyzed the evolution from an agrarian society regulated by the sun and the changing seasons to an industrial society regimented by the routine of the factory whistle.

Cotton Mills, Lowell, Massachusetts. Once located primarily in New England, now cotton mills are found in the Cotton Belt.

Boott Cotton Mills Museum, Lowell, Massachusetts.

Beginning in the mid-18th century, a succession of English inventions—notably the flying shuttle, the spinning jenny, and the Arkwright frame—remade the textile industry. To protect the British hegemony, Parliament banned the export of the new technology as well as the emigration of persons skilled in its design or operation.

Samuel Slater, who had risen from apprentice to superintendent of an English textile mill, broke this embargo on know-how. Superintendent was as high as he could aspire in the social stratification of England; but there was less class rigidity across the ocean. In 1789, after memorizing the design of the Arkwright frame, he pretended to be a farmer and sailed for New England. Four years later, he and his partners built the first water-powered cotton mill in North America, in Pawtucket, Rhode Island.

The success of Slater and those who followed him inspired wealthy New England shipping families to shift their capital into manufacturing, which provided more secure returns. Francis Cabot Lowell of Boston realized that a truly lucrative textile industry required efficient power looms—still an English monopoly. He toured English mills and committed the details of such machines to memory. Back home, he and mechanic Paul Moody perfected the idea and built their own looms. They installed them in their new, integrated factory—the entire process of textile production under one roof—in Waltham, Massachusetts, in 1814. Their system quickly spread throughout southern New England, where there was an abundance of fast-running streams to provide waterpower. Towns like Woonsocket, Rhode Island, and Lowell, Massachusetts, boomed.

The introduction of the power loom permitted a major change in the workforce. With all stages of production under a single roof and the physical ease of operating a power loom, the former reliance on family labor gave way to factories staffed by women. Single women, usually aged 15 to 25, left their rural homes in numbers far beyond what domestic service could accommodate and earned wages that allowed them to put something by. In keeping with the prevailing mores, they lived in tightly supervised dormitories and led an enforced prim and proper existence; "Lowell girls" were a byword for decades. After an average of three years in the mills, these girls married, migrated west, found less burdensome jobs, or went back to the farm.

> Cotton fibers flatten and twist naturally as they dry. At mills the fibers are carded, combed, and spun.

As time passed and the reservoir of rural workers was depleted, immigrants—first Irish, later Italians, Jews, and others—replaced them in the lowest-paying jobs, altering the character of American cities forever.

The machinery in the mills had to be built and maintained. The expertise accumulated thereby spawned a host of industries producing machines for agricultural and home use—inventions that improved the quality of life for the new and expanding middle class.

The cotton textile industry was the first to decline. Toward the end of the 19th century, when electricity replaced waterpower, mill-owners began relocating their plants to southern states where wages and taxes were lower, unions unknown, and laws protecting workers weak or nonexistent. This was a foretaste of what happened in other industries after World War II, and again in textiles in the last quarter of the 20th century, when the mills abandoned the American South for Third World countries.

New England Churches
Religious Faith & Community Heart

New Hampshire, Connecticut, Rhode Island, and Massachusetts

From the very beginning, religion set the tone for American life. Dissenters fleeing persecution by the established church in England settled New England. In the New World they instituted a regime that drew no clear line between church government and civil government. In Massachusetts Bay, the civil franchise was originally limited to church members in good standing. In fact, in most towns and villages the church was also the community meeting house.

Anglicanism was the established church in the Carolinas, Virginia, and Maryland. Full freedom of conscience for all creeds existed only in Pennsylvania, founded by Quakers, and in Rhode Island.

Jonathan Edwards, known as the "theologian of the heart" in colonial America and abroad, was the moving spirit of the Great Awakening of the early 1740s. Edwards emphasized God's sovereignty, human depravity, the reality of hell, and the need for spiritual rebirth. If America could preserve its essential moral purity, he said, the millennium would commence in the New World.

As early as the 16th century, Catholic missionaries from Spain and France sought converts to Christianity among the native tribes of the western and northern frontiers.

St. Anne, Sturbridge, Massachusetts. New England churches like this one formed the core of many communities. French Canadians and the Irish came to Fiskdale to work in the Fiske textile mills. Built in 1883, St. Anne served French-speaking families, while St. Patrick served the Irish. In 1887, they were combined into a single parish.

Edwards's revivalism cost him his pulpit and did not keep New England Calvinism from splitting into evangelical and rationalist streams. Leaders of the latter camp rejected the emotional component of the Great Awakening. Confident of the human capacity to know and do God's will, they rejected Calvinist notions of innate human depravity and predestination. During the second half of the 18th century this camp evolved into American Unitarianism, which proclaims that all human beings have the capacity to redeem themselves.

In most colonial towns and villages, the church was also the community meeting house.

Few of America's founding fathers were deeply religious. Raised in the Enlightenment, they valued rational inquiry and rejected religious enthusiasm. Religion was praiseworthy because it provided a solid basis for moral conduct, but it was to be achieved by rational insight, not imposed by government fiat. For Washington, freedom of conscience was an "inherent natural right." He was proud, he said, to live in a country where "every person may worship God according to the dictates of his own heart."

This widespread sentiment is why the principle of religious noncoercion was enshrined in the First Amendment, which, by banning any "establishment of religion," ensured that different accounts of the truth would be able to compete freely in the marketplace of ideas and sentiments. Although the First Amendment applied only to the Federal government, every state soon ended tax support for churches and eventually abolished religious tests for voting and office holding.

In 1775, only one American in twenty belonged to a church. The 19th century, however, brought a wave of religious revival, known as the Second Great Awakening, that continued until the Civil War. Its inception is traditionally placed at Cane Ridge in central Kentucky. There, on August 6–12, 1801, dozens of Presbyterian, Baptist, and Methodist clergymen and 20,000 to 30,000 laypeople of all ages and social classes engaged in an intense, day-and-night religious experience of hymn-singing, public confession, personal witness, and collective prayer, accompanied by fiery sermons. The meeting broke up only when the participants ran out of food. Over the next six months, 100,000 Kentuckians were attracted to the movement. By 1811, 3 to 4 million Americans were attending camp meetings each year.

The rituals of this evangelical religion—camp meetings, group prayer, and mass outdoor baptisms—were a crucial part of American identity in the decades before the Civil War. One of its key tenets was that individuals were duty-bound to fight their own sinful nature and could win the battle.

Just as the Puritans in Massachusetts had seen themselves as the spearhead of a struggle to reform all Protestantism, 19th century American evangelicals viewed themselves as the vanguard of a spiritual movement to make Christian morality the center of daily life, in the United States and then the entire world. Carrying on Jonathan Edwards's idea that the millennium would begin in the New World, they set out to reform American society. America, they believed, was God's chosen vessel for the redemption of the world.

The Second Great Awakening swelled the ranks of the Methodist and Baptist churches; it also produced new sects like the Cumberland Presbyterians, the Christian Church, and the Disciples of Christ, and attracted new converts to groups like the Shakers.

With the Great Awakening the number of church members doubled between 1800 and 1840. The churches that had dominated the colonial era—Congregationalist, Anglican-Episcopalian, and Presbyterian—stagnated while other denominations expanded rapidly: Baptist congregations from 400 in 1780 to over 12,000 in 1860; Methodist churches from 50 to 20,000; Roman Catholic churches from 50 to 2,500. By 1860, Irish and German immigrants helped bring the Catholic population to 3 million, the largest religious denomination in the country.

Church in Grafton, Vermont. Across America churches have formed the core of the community. In them people found support and nourishment of the shared values and ideals. For more than 225 years, in churches, synagogues, temples, and mosques, people have met to affirm their faith and identity both as a religious people and as Americans. © Corbis.

New religious sects, the Mormons, Seventh-Day Adventists, Jehovah's Witnesses, and Christian Scientists also grew in the 19th century. The Mormons, founded by Joseph Smith, who proclaimed, "Zion will be built upon this [the North American] continent," eventually led followers to Utah. Neighbors feared them as bloc voters subservient to elders, and their practice of polygamy was considered a threat to the social order.

The conflict between traditionalists and rationalists in the Christian church cost Jonathan Edwards his pastorate and can be traced through American history. Today's 20th century descendants of Second Great Awakening converts were drawn into a Fundamentalist revival even while Unitarians and Episcopalians have pursued an increasingly liberal agenda. Since the early 1900s, most Americans, conservative and liberal, have believed that the United States has a mission to lead the world in a golden age of freedom and equality. America has become the most church-going nation in the Western world.

MOSQUES

Islam, perhaps the most misunderstood religion in America, is based upon a strict monotheism and encourages peace, achieved through its followers' direct relationship with God. The roots of Islam in America go as far back as the Transatlantic slave trade; many West Coast Africans were of the Islamic faith. Centuries later, many African-Americans have rediscovered this faith. Islam in America embraces the basic values of the founding fathers and a belief in freedom, justice, and equality. The teachings of Imam W. Deen Mohammed, leader of the largest indigenous community of American Muslims, affirm this. America's religious freedom has enabled not just African-Americans, but Muslims in many established as well as immigrant American communities from Turkey, Indonesia, Afghanistan, and all parts of the world, to worship freely and openly in American cities and towns. In 2002, the Muslim community of Dearborn, Michigan, the largest Islamic community in America, began construction on the largest mosque in North America.

HUDSON RIVER

Knickerbocker Tales: How New Netherland Became New York

"Nothing could be more beautiful than our passage down the Hudson [River].... The change, the contrast, the ceaseless variety of beauty, as you skim from side to side, the liquid smoothness of the broad mirror which reflects the scene, and most of all, the clear bright air through which you look at it."
—Frances Trollope (1832)

The Hudson River, about 315 miles long, was a major route for American Indians and Dutch and English traders and settlers. At its mouth grew one of the world's largest and busiest harbors. During the Revolutionary War, American colonists fought the British over its possession. When the Erie Canal was finished in 1825, linking the Hudson with the Great Lakes, Manhattan's prosperity was assured.

FROM LAKE TEAR OF THE CLOUDS IN THE ADIRONDACKS TO NEW YORK BAY Verrazzano, Hudson, and other early explorers were not really interested in the North American continent. They were actually looking for a Northwest Passage to the wealth of the East Indies. What they found, but did not recognize, was what eventually became one of the richest places in the New World—New York harbor and the Hudson River.

In 1609, Henry Hudson, an Englishman employed by the Dutch East India Company, thought he had found the Northwest Passage when he discovered a broad inlet running north past what was later named Manhattan Island. He sailed up it for 150 miles, past the site of present-day Albany, before realizing his mistake. For his troubles and error, however, he got the river named for him.

Roundout Lighthouse, Kingston, New York. Courtesy of © Ulster County Tourism.

Hudson River. Courtesy of © Ulster County Tourism.

The Dutch decided, with typical Dutch practicality, that if there was no Northwest Passage they would settle for what there was. A decade later the Dutch founded the colony of New Netherland. In 1626 the newly formed West India Company purchased Manhattan Island and established the settlement of New Amsterdam. The town itself was populated by bourgeois; large tracts of land along the river were granted to quasi-feudal patroons, who, in return for bringing over fifty adults within a four-year period, enjoyed exclusive fishing and hunting rights, civil and criminal jurisdiction, a share of the fur trade, and one-third of their tenants' crops.

The English seized the Dutch holdings in 1664 and renamed the colony New York, but the patrician landowners and their tenants were left in possession. Their Dutch family names—including Van Buren, Vanderbilt, and Roosevelt—were passed down through the generations.

The Atlantic coast of English America has comparatively few navigable rivers that penetrate any significant distance into the interior. The Hudson is the most important exception: seagoing vessels can ascend as far as Albany; smaller vessels can continue as far as Troy (150 miles upstream from Manhattan) and some distance up the Mohawk. In the era when waterborne transportation was faster and cheaper than overland conveyances, this spurred the development of upper New York State.

House on Hudson, Ulster County, New York.
Courtesy of © Ulster County Tourism.

Washington Irving was one of the first American writers to be recognized at home and abroad. His stories of Sancte Claus helped define the cozy American Christmas ritual.

Other literary talents were drawn to New York by its growing literary interest and opportunity. With wealth and population came the means for patronage of culture. By 1820, most leading booksellers and printers were in Manhattan.

During the Revolutionary War, the British plan to occupy the Hudson Valley and sever New England from the Middle Atlantic colonies failed when Burgoyne surrendered at Saratoga in October 1777. After this, George Washingon decided that West Point, on the west bank of the Hudson fifty miles upstream of Manhattan, was the most strategically significant position in the entire country. After having fortifications built there he assigned Benedict Arnold, whose military abilities he highly esteemed, to command the vital post. Arnold's plot to deliver the fortress to the English was discovered by chance and foiled. West Point, where the U.S. Military Academy was established in the early 19th century, is the oldest continuously occupied military base in the United States.

Robert Fulton's introduction of the steamboat in 1807 was a boon to the already booming river commerce on the Hudson. By 1850 some 150 steamers, carrying a million passengers a year, were plying the route. The Erie Canal, completed in 1825 and linking the Hudson with the Great Lakes, still wasn't the Northwest Passage to the Indies—but it proved far more valuable, opening the Midwest and great American heartland to trade with the East Coast and Europe. The Hudson River became one of the most important commercial arteries in the world and New York City, at its mouth, one of the busiest ports in the world.

The Hudson River appears in Washington Irving's *Sketch Book* (1819), which includes "The Legend of Sleepy Hollow," "Rip Van Winkle," and other stories. The Knickerbockers—named after Diedrich Knickerbocker, the supposed author of Washington Irving's fictional *A History of New York....* (1812)—were early 19th century Manhattan young men of Dutch and English stock of mercantile and landed families who easily mingled in the freedom of New World society. Irving's book is both a burlesque of history books and a political satire.

THE HUDSON RIVER SCHOOL

The Hudson River School, a group of painters (1825–1875), began to devote themselves to landscape painting rather than portraiture and were attracted by the beauty of the Hudson River valley, Niagara Falls, the Catskills, and the White Mountains. The work of these artists reflected a new concept of beautiful and not fearsome wilderness in which people were insignificant. New York became a principal art center, especially after the formation of the National Academy of Design in 1828. After 1830 few great portrait painters, like Copley and Stuart, remained.

CUMBERLAND GAP
Appalachian Gateway to the West

MIDDLESBORO, KENTUCKY; HARROGATE, TENNESSEE; AND SOUTHWESTERN VIRGINIA

The end of the French and Indian War, in 1763, found 1.5 million people living between the Atlantic and the Appalachians. A Royal Proclamation of that year barred European settlement west of the mountains. This policy aggravated two groups of colonials whose interests were otherwise antithetical: seaboard planters and merchants who wanted to devote their surplus cash to land speculation, and backwoodsmen looking for new plow land to support their expanding population.

Even Lord Dunmore, the royal governor of Virginia, ignored the ban: he needed land for discharged soldiers. Dunmore sent a party of surveyors down the Ohio River in 1773. One of its members, James Harrod, returned the next year and mapped the future site of Louisville. Then he and his team went up the Kentucky River and founded the first permanent English settlement west of the Allegheny Mountains—Harrodsburg.

Of the many groups of investors that tried to acquire land in the western wilderness, only one—that headed by Col. Richard Henderson of North Carolina—is remembered today, chiefly because he hired Daniel Boone

Hensley Settlement, Cumberland National Historical Park, Kentucky, Tennessee, and Virginia. From 1750 to 1830, many Americans packed their belongings on horses, in covered wagons, and on their backs and found their way west through the Cumberland Gap to settle in lands beyond the Appalachian Mountains. This mountain pass, 1,304 feet high, borders on three states: Virginia, Tennessee, and Kentucky. It passes through a ridge of the Cumberlands from southeast of Middlesboro, Kentucky to northeast Tennessee. © William A. Bake/Corbis.

to implement his scheme. Boone, born in Pennsylvania in 1734, migrated to the North Carolina frontier in his youth. In his thirties, bitten by the exploration bug, he began ranging farther afield. On June 7, 1769, a fur trader named John Finley guided him through Cumberland Gap.

Even without royal proclamations and hostile natives, the mountain ridge running from New York to Alabama posed a formidable barrier to westward travel. The first white man to render a written report about a passable route through the Appalachians was Thomas Walker, a Virginia physician who turned to exploration and passed through Cumberland Gap into Kentucky in 1750. The Gap, carved over millennia by wind and water, had long served as a migration path for game animals and the American Indian hunters who followed them.

Kentucky, the "dark and bloody ground" of warfare among the native tribes, was unpopulated, a hunting reserve and buffer zone between the Cherokee, Creek, and Chickasaw in the south, and the Shawnee and Wyandot in the north. The vacuum attracted European settlers, who were fiercely resisted by natives defending their hunting rights. In 1774 the Virginia militia trounced the Shawnee, who thereupon ceded their claims to Kentucky.

In March 1775 the Cherokee, reading the handwriting on the wall, deeded the territory between the Ohio, Kentucky, and Cumberland rivers to Henderson's Transylvania Company. In the largest private or corporate land deal in American history, more than 20 million acres of land were sold for 2,000 pounds sterling and goods worth 8,000 pounds.

Henderson had already sent Boone and 28 men to mark out a trail from what is now Kingsport, Tennessee, through the Cumberland Gap to the Kentucky River, where they established the settlement of Boonesboro. With the road open, the trickle of white adventurers turned into a flood of families. By 1780, some 50 separate "stations," several of them sizable communities protected by wooden palisades, had been established. Although many settlers (including Boone's oldest son) died in Indian raids and massacres, people kept pouring through the Gap—an estimated 70,000 to 100,000 by the time Kentucky was admitted to the Union in 1792, some 300,000 by 1810.

The route was officially named Wilderness Road in 1796, when the narrow trail was widened to accommodate wagons. From about 1830 Wilderness Road fell into disuse, as better highways were constructed. After that Cumberland Gap was little traveled until U.S.–25 was built through it in the 1920s. In the 1990s twin tunnels removed the highway from the surface, restoring the Gap to something like the natural state in which Walker and Boone had first seen it.

MISSISSIPPI RIVER

Father of Waters

"The basin of the Mississippi is the Body of the Nation. All the other parts are but members, important in themselves, yet more important in their relations to this."—Harper's Magazine (February 1863); epigraph for Mark Twain's *Life on the Mississippi* (1883)

FLOWS FROM MINNESOTA, WISCONSIN, IOWA, ILLINOIS, KENTUCKY, MISSOURI, ARKANSAS, TENNESSEE, MISSISSIPPI, DOWN TO LOUISIANA

The Mississippi—"father of waters" in the Algonquian languages—flows some 2,350 miles from its source in Lake Itasca, Minnesota, south to the Gulf of Mexico. Its watershed of 1,250,000 square miles, third largest in the world, covers two-fifths of the area of the contiguous states.

The northern section of the river—from the head of navigation at St. Paul south to St. Louis—is often omitted from the collective image of the Mississippi. But the river and its tributaries are central to the economy, topography, and life of Minnesota, Wisconsin, Illinois, and Iowa no less than to those of the states from Missouri south to the Gulf.

Tall bluffs on the banks border the upper Mississippi. Seduced by river-borne commerce, the towns have expanded into the narrow flood plain at their base. But the hinterland—home, in Mark Twain's words, to "an independent race who think for themselves,...educated and enlightened"—overlooks the river from a safe height. The upper river, walled up in a narrow channel that does not vary, is serious and businesslike, constant and dependable. Life here has its verities: Iowa is always west of the river, Illinois east of it.

Mark Twain *riverboat, Hannibal, Missouri.*

Tom Sawyer's white fence, Hannibal, Missouri.

South of Cairo, Illinois, where the Ohio River flows into the Mississippi, the situation is quite different. Here the river flows through a broad valley (40–70 miles) that was once an inlet of the Gulf of Mexico. This alluvial estuary has been filled in by silt over the eons, extending the Mississippi southward by more than 600 miles. The river flows between natural levees, beyond which stretch broad and fertile floodplains. The Mississippi meanders in slow curves, in no hurry to reach the Gulf: it flows more than twice as far as a crow flies to get from Cairo to New Orleans. In this soft soil the channel is always shifting. Sometimes the Mississippi cuts through narrow necks, straightening and shortening its course—leaving riverside communities on a backwater or several miles inland, isolating pieces of Mississippi or Tennessee on the Louisiana or Arkansas bank, or viceversa. It is not just the river that, as Heraclitus knew, is never the same river. Along the lower Mississippi, the land, too, never stays the same for long. But the river is always there, its floods bringing the rich black soil that supports the cotton plantations and a culture very different from that of the upper valley.

The Mississippi was the main transportation artery of the central United States—one-way in the early days, two-way after the invention of the steamboat. The first steamboat came downriver to New Orleans in 1812. At the peak of the antebellum boom, when Mark Twain was a riverman, an average of 3,000 paddle wheelers called on the city each year.

Twain never forgot his youth on the river, that "wonderful book…[with] a new story to tell every day." He himself told one of the best, creating a classic metaphor of the American experience in *Huckleberry Finn*, the tale of a white boy and a black man on a raft floating down the Mississippi, in search of freedom and self-knowledge.

French explorers, like Louis Jolliet and Father Marquette, left St. Ignace, in the Michigan upper peninsula, in search of the legendary "messipi" described by the Indians. After a month, their canoes, following a river, were swept into the Mississippi, which they rode to the mouth of the Arkansas River before it became clear that they had failed to find a water route to the Pacific.

"The Mississippi River will always have its own way; no engineering skill can persuade it to do otherwise…"
—Mark Twain in Bernard DeVotos, Ed., *Mark Twain in Eruption* (1940)

About the water, Mark Twain said in Life on the Mississippi *(1883), "It is good for steamboating, and good to drink; but it is worthless for all other purposes, except baptizing."*

NEW ORLEANS

Louisiana Territory & Birthplace of Jazz

THE FRENCH QUARTER, NEW ORLEANS, LOUISIANA

In 1718, Jean Baptiste Le Moyne established a settlement on the Mississippi about 110 miles upstream from the Gulf of Mexico, on the southern shore of Lake Pontchartrain, and named it Nouvelle Orleans. At the time, France controlled Canada and claimed Louisiana, the vast watershed of the Mississippi, and hoped to exploit their resources through the newly established port. But no more than a trickle of French subjects emigrated to Canada, while Louisiana attracted even fewer. After the loss of Canada and the Ohio Valley to Britain in 1763, hold-

Eighteenth century Indian trade was a key to expanding empires in North America. The French of Louisiana were better traders with the Indians than were the Spanish of New Mexico and the British of Carolina.

French Quarter, New Orleans, Louisiana. Early 18th century trade was in cotton, fur, lead, hemp, tobacco, and molasses. The town was filled with glamour, drunkenness, gold, murder, and romance. According to historian Robert M. Coates in The Outlaw Years (1930), *the city had "blanketed Indians, garlanded Creoles, trappers in buckskins and red-shirted flatboatmen," as well as pig-tailed mariners, slaves, and laughing girls, whose caresses money could buy.*

ABOVE: *Mississippi riverboat, the Natchez, docked at New Orleans. New Orleans was called the Crescent City, because it was built on the great bend of the Mississippi River.* BELOW: *Statue of Louis Armstrong, Armstrong Park, New Orleans National Jazz Park, New Orleans, Louisiana.*

Jazz, a uniquely American art form, was born in the 19th century, influenced by African-American work songs, field shouts, sorrow songs, hymns, and spirituals. It also used rhythmic, harmonic, and melodic elements from the blues and from French and Spanish Creole roots. To some listeners, its spontaneous, emotional, and improvisational character suggested loose morals and low life. But jazz soon found a wider audience and spread from New Orleans to Chicago, Kansas City, New York, and the West Coast.

ing the territory was not worthwhile, so Louisiana was ceded to Spain. New Orleans' prosperity began during the 40 years of Spanish control.

Although the French drew up the plan for the original town, the architecture of today's Vieux Carré, or French Quarter, is Spanish. Devastating fires in 1788 and 1794 destroyed everything older. The architectural hallmarks of the French Quarter, rear courtyards and wrought-iron balconies, are actually Iberian touches.

At first Spain allowed the Anglo-American colonizers of the Ohio Valley to trade through New Orleans. By the time Spain grew alarmed and tried to limit their privileges, it was too late. When he became president, Thomas Jefferson realized the importance of New Orleans and set about to acquire that vital city. When Napoleon, who had reclaimed Louisiana from Spain, offered the entire territory to the United States, Jefferson snapped up the bargain. In December 1803, the Stars and Stripes was raised over New Orleans.

Two milestones were reached in 1812: Louisiana was admitted to the Union and the first steamboat reached New Orleans. The decades that followed were the city's golden age. It grew faster than any other large city in the country, despite hurricanes, epidemics, and the enervating heat and humidity. Its French-speaking Catholic society gave it a flavor quite unlike the rest of the country, epitomized in its annual Mardi Gras celebration (starting in 1827) and vibrant musical life. In 1840 it was the third largest American city (only 120 people behind Baltimore) and the fourth busiest port in the world, transshipping millions of dollars' worth of cotton and sugar each year.

New Orleans was the only town in the South that attracted immigrants: in 1860, they composed almost half its white population. But its southern-ness was reflected in the fact that its economy was based almost exclusively on commerce and shipping, with little or no industry.

Then came the Civil War. The people of New Orleans, with their strong commercial ties to the upper Mississippi and Ohio Valleys, were overwhelmingly opposed to secession but were outvoted by the rest of Louisiana.

Union forces occupied New Orleans in April 1862. River commerce resumed after the fall of Vicksburg and Port Hudson the following July. New Orleans, however, never retrieved its former prominence. The railroads cut into its importance as a shipping center, cotton was dethroned, and the Industrial Revolution enriched other sectors of the country.

What now made it unique, though, was its African-American society, both pre-war free blacks, or Creoles of mixed French or Spanish and African descent, and emancipated slaves. Creoles, with their French or Spanish language and culture, looked down on the freed slaves. But the rise of Jim Crow equalized their disabilities and forced them to live together.

The musical encounter between the Creoles and the freedmen and freedwomen produced a musical form that could have arisen only in New Orleans: jazz. All the great names of the first decades of jazz, including Buddy Bolden, Jelly Roll Morton, and "King" Oliver, lived and worked there. Later, when jazz conquered the country and then the world, its most famous interpreter was another son of New Orleans, Louis Armstrong.

> ### CAJUNS
> In the 18th century, with France and England almost constantly at war, French-speaking Acadians were exiled from what had become British Nova Scotia. By the mid-1760s, many relocated to Louisiana, where they were welcomed by the colony's new Spanish government. Acadians settled in southern Louisiana in isolated bayous and became what today we call Cajuns. Their contribution to Louisiana culture, music, and cuisine supplies part of New Orleans's distinctive spice.

> New Orleans was founded by the sieur de Bienville in 1718. In 1722 it became the French colony capital and soon grew into a major port. The secret Treaty of Fontainebleau (1762), confirmed in the Treaty of Paris (1763), transferred Louisiana to Spain. From its position on the Mississippi River delta, New Orleans could control river traffic into the Gulf of Mexico. The city was briefly returned to the French
>
>
>
> before the United States acquired it with the 1803 Louisiana Purchase. Creole culture dominated the Big Easy until the late 19th century, and its French roots are still felt today.

LEWIS & CLARK'S TRAIL TO THE PACIFIC

Expedition with Sacajawea, Indian Guide

"The object of your mission is to explore the Missouri River, and such principal streams of it, as, by its course and communication with the waters of the Pacific Ocean, whether the Columbia, Oregan, Colorado, or any other river, may offer the most direct and practible water-communication across the continent, for the purposes of commerce."—Thomas Jefferson, letter to Meriwether Lewis, June 20, 1803

MISSOURI, KANSAS, ILLINOIS, IOWA, SOUTH DAKOTA, NORTH DAKOTA, MONTANA, IDAHO, OREGON, WASHINGTON

The early maritime explorers of North America were looking for the Northwest Passage, a shortcut to the fabled riches of the Orient. The greatest overland journey of exploration on that continent was also looking for a "northwest passage." But since its initiator was Thomas Jefferson, the leading polymath in American history, that was only one goal of Meriwether Lewis, William Clark, and their party as they traveled up the Missouri River and westward to the Pacific.

In addition to looking for the "most direct and practible [practicable] water communication across this continent, for the purposes of commerce," Jefferson instructed them to study the people, flora, fauna, and minerals along their route. To facilitate this, Jefferson sent Lewis, his private secretary, to Philadelphia, the scientific capital of the young nation, to study botany, mathematics, mineralogy, chemistry, and other subjects. To interest native tribes in peaceful interactions with the easterners, they were to exchange both goods and knowledge. (Jefferson specifically mentioned the then-new technique of cowpox vaccination.)

Jefferson also had a political motive—the British were beginning to show an interest in the Pacific Northwest. Originally the expedition was a secret, because America west of the Mississippi was under Spanish

Scenic Overlook of Missouri River valley from Council Bluffs, Iowa. Here, on their journey to the Northwest, Lewis and Clark met the Otoe and Missouria Indians. On his map of their journey, Lewis marked the place "CB," Council Bluffs.

THE LEWIS AND CLARK TRAIL (1804–1806)

control. In the spring of 1803, however, Napoleon, who had retrieved the province from Spain, agreed to sell Louisiana (the watershed of the Mississippi and its western tributaries) to the United States for $12 million. This gave the expedition another purpose—exploring the vast territory acquired by the United States and introducing the new sovereign to its American Indian residents.

Lewis set out from Pittsburgh in August 1803. In Louisville he met Clark, an old friend whom he had chosen as his co-commander. Their party of thirty-odd sailed down the Ohio and spent the winter of 1803–1804 at Wood River, Illinois, where the Missouri joins the Mississippi. On May 14, 1804, they began their ascent of the partially explored Missouri in three boats. In October they reached Mandan territory in present-day North Dakota and encamped for the winter.

Here they hired a trapper named Toussaint Charbonneau and his Shoshone wife, Sacajawea (or Sacagawea), to serve as interpreters in the uncharted lands to the west. In addition to her fluency in the native languages, they valued Sacajawea's presence as a token of their peaceful intentions.

In April of 1805 they set out again, reaching the Great Falls of the Missouri River in mid-summer. After a difficult portage around that obstacle, they attained the head of navigation in August and abandoned their boats. As luck would have it, the chief of the Shoshone band whom Lewis encountered in his quest for horses was Sacajawea's long-lost brother. Exhausted and hungry after crossing the Rockies on the Shoshone horses, they were rescued by friendly Nez Percés. When they came to a westward-flowing stream they built new boats, knowing they were almost "home." In mid-November they reached the Pacific coast at the mouth of the Columbia River.

The return journey, which began the following March, ended in St. Louis on September 23, 1806, capping a journey of more than 8,000 miles. After stopovers in their Louisville and Charlottesville homes, Clark and Lewis continued to Washington and meetings with President Jefferson. They had crossed the continent from ocean to ocean.

Clark's maps and journals, plus the many specimens the explorers brought back, were the immediate harvest of the expedition. In later decades, their encampment at the mouth of the Columbia was an important component of the United States' claim to the Pacific Northwest. Above all, there was the young republic's symbolic assertion of dominion over the entire continent, coast to coast—the harbinger of the concept of manifest destiny that shaped its history for the next half-century.

TRAILS WEST

Covered Wagons, Rolling Homes of Pioneers

ROADS, TRAILS, TRACES, AND PATHS WEST

The covered wagon has become the icon of the second great wave of westward expansion, which brought pioneers from the Mississippi Valley across the Great Plains, mountains, and desert, via the Santa Fe and Oregon Trails, to California and the Pacific Northwest between the 1830s and the Civil War. During these three decades, more than 300,000 Americans followed these routes in search of new homes and economic security. Many, if not most, traveled in canvas-covered wagons whose design could be traced to the second decade of the 18th century and the Conestoga Valley of southeastern Pennsylvania.

This Conestoga wagon dates from about 1790. The covered wagon, prairie schooner, and Conestoga wagon were temporary homes to many people moving West to reestablish their lives on the frontier.

TRAILS WEST IN THE MID-1880s

A few of the many trails West include the Old Spanish Trail, Natchez Trace, Old National Road, Oregon Trail, California Trail, Gila Trail, Bozeman Trail, and Santa Fe Trail.

The Conestoga wagon was the heavy truck of its day, before the advent of canals and railroads. The typical Conestoga, pulled by four to six horses, might reach 25 feet long and a tare weight of 1½ tons.

The Conestoga is a good example of how function begets form. In addition to the trademark arched cover—originally hemp, later a double layer of cotton that could repel all but the heaviest downpours—it featured a box that was bowed in one or both directions, to prevent cargo from shifting on inclines, and caulked so that it could float across larger streams. It had large iron-rimmed wheels, broad enough to support the heavily laden wagon over soft or muddy ground and high enough (4 feet or more) to keep the box above fordable watercourses and pass over obstacles like stumps, rocks, and ruts.

The Santa Fe Trail was the principal trade route to and from California for two decades, until the completion of the transcontinental railway in 1869. Freight haulers along this route appreciated the advantages of the Conestoga but usually replaced the horses with mules, which were hardier animals and better able to endure the arid conditions of the Southwest, including the menacingly named Death Valley.

A typical wagon train consisted of 25 wagons, which lumbered along at an average speed of one to two miles an hour and made about 100 miles in a seven-day week (provisions were too sparse to allow for rest days en route).

On the Oregon Trail, traversed by more people and less cargo, the Conestoga's size made it impracticable. Pioneers downsized it to create the prairie schooner (or prairie wagon), whose bed was typically 4 feet wide and 10 to 12 feet long. Standing some 10 feet to the top of its canvas bonnet, it weighed only 1,300 pounds empty and could be pulled by teams of four to six oxen or six to ten mules.

Santa Fe Trail, Dodge City, Kansas. The trail began on the west bank of the Missouri river and led west to Fort Dodge, Kansas, where it forked, one route going southwest and one going west. Tracks can still be seen on the trail.

Many pioneering families could not afford to buy a prairie schooner because its construction required a skilled wainwright and a large number of draft animals were needed to pull it. So they simply fitted their farm wagons with a bonnet to keep out rain, sun, and dust and set out.

The journey took four to six months, much of it during blistering hot and dry summers. But being caught in a winter blizzard, as occurred to the Donner Party in northern California in 1846–1847, was almost a sure death warrant.

During its two busiest decades, 1835–1855, at least 10,000 pioneers perished along the Oregon Trail, victims of accidents and disease. Although the native peoples were never enthusiastic about the travelers who were crossing their land, the popular image of incessant attacks on wagon trains is overblown. The nighttime "circling the wagons" was mainly to protect against wild animals and make it harder for little children to wander off. The best estimates are that, on average, Indians killed only 20 to 25 pioneers each year during those two decades.

"The so-called Santa Fe Trail was just a wheel track in the grass, no road, no bridges across the creek and rivers...We traveled the trail 14 miles a day [for] 2 months...New Mexico, now the fourth largest state in the union, was many hundreds of miles away to the south with no roads, many rivers without bridges, just the Santa Fe trail. The trail was nothing but a wagon wheel mark in the tall grass. I was going to a land of blue sky and a lazy, shiftless town of Mex King. The Spaniards had been there since they landed on this continent, settled there in 1600. They called the land Pues Tiempo—*the land of 'Pretty Soon,' and the inhabitants lived up to their motto. Never do anything today that you can do tomorrow—The Americans called it the land of Rip Van Winkle."*—Frank Dermott, early traveler (about 1821) on the Santa Fe Trail

LOG CABINS & SOD HOUSES
Frontier Settlers & Hopeful Homesteaders

AMERICAN FRONTIER

T he colony of New Sweden is a minor blip on the screen of American history. Only sixteen years elapsed from its founding in 1638 at the mouth of the Delaware River (near present-day Wilmington) until its annexation by the Dutch in 1654. But the few hundred Swedes and Finns who settled there left a major imprint on subsequent American history. For it was they who brought the log cabin to the New World.

The English settlers of Virginia, New England, and the Middle Colonies did not employ this type of housing during the 17th century. But the Scotch-Irish, who began immigrating in large numbers after 1718 and moved out to the western fringes of the settled land, took to it readily. In part this was because they had been accustomed to similar rude dwellings back home in the Lowlands and northern Ireland.

Old Pioneer Cabin, Colonel Heg Memorial Park, Waterford, Wisconsin. This log cabin served the Halvor Benedickson family of nine as home for several years after the parents immigrated from Norway in the 1840s.

Howard Pioneer School, Log Cabin Village, Fort Worth, Texas. Hartsford Howard was born in 1819 in Georgia. He married Susan C. Niblack in 1845 and they had eight children. Built on the Texas frontier, this cabin saw its share of gun play. On one occasion, the young son, Billay Howard, drove off an Indian attack by firing from the upstairs windows of this cabin until help arrived. The cabin was remodeled in 1995 to depict a typical one-room school with living quarters for the teacher on the second floor.

But it was also because the log cabin was ideal for the frontier. It required only squared logs and mud daubing, no nails, and no more tools than a sharp axe. A man working alone could put up a one-room cabin with a floor of hard-packed dirt in the space of a week. Log cabins were more fire-resistant, warmer in winter, and drier in wet weather than board construction, and they did not have to be painted.

Stripped to the basics, cabins were rough dwellings, quick and inexpensive to build and hence, readily abandoned without tears—just the style appropriate for the seminomadic pioneers in their insecure frontier clearings.

Once they did find a place to settle down, though, frontier families didn't want to stay in a one-room cabin any longer than necessary. Their goal was to build a new frame or stone house as soon as they could afford one. Only the poorest backwoods families were unable to "move up," though they might improve the structure by adding board siding or plaster.

The log cabin became a powerful symbol of the frontier in its social, economic, and political opposition to the East. As such it featured prominently in the authorized biographies and presidential campaigns of the earliest backwoods politicians to gain national prominence, including Andrew Jackson, Davy Crockett, and William Henry Harrison. Harrison had actually been born on a Virginia plantation, son of a former governor, and was no backwoodsman at all. However, the symbol helped him win the 1840 elections over the "aristocratic" incumbent Martin Van Buren, who was in fact the son of a farmer and tavern keeper. Abraham Lincoln, the successful railroad lawyer, evoked his birth in a Kentucky log cabin to distinguish himself from the eastern politicians who competed against him for the Republican nomination in 1860. (Jefferson Davis was also born in a Kentucky log cabin but did not play up this fact.)

After the Civil War, the log cabin faded from public view (Garfield was the last president born in one). The new frontier of the Great Plains was treeless; its characteristic provisional dwelling was the sod house or soddie, inspired by the earth lodges of the sedentary native tribes of the region. Soddies are sturdy, but not as robust as log cabins, and they were replaced by frame or brick construction as soon as the pioneers' financial situation and access (thanks to the railroad) to lumber made it possible. Few were built or occupied after the end of the 19th century.

The log cabin, which with minimal maintenance can last a human lifetime, had a longer career. As late as 1939, 270,000 log cabins were being used as primary dwellings in the United States, most of them in the southern Appalachians and Ozark Mountains.

ONE-ROOM SCHOOLHOUSE
Universal Education, Essential to a Democracy

FRONTIER, RURAL, AND SMALL-TOWN AMERICA

Washington Irving's description of Ichabod Crane presiding over the one-room schoolhouse, with "pupils' voices, conning over their lessons...like the hum of a beehive; interrupted now and then by the authoritative voice of the master, in the tone of menace or command..." in "The Legend of Sleepy Hollow" (1819) faithfully represents the institution. Fifty years later when a fictional Tom Sawyer attended school in a Missouri small town, girls, seated separately, were among the scholars. In the 19th century, most rural and small-town schools held twenty to fifty students, nearly all from respectable middle-class families. In a single room, one row of desks was for each of the eight grades. Many teachers, just a few years older than their pupils and with a year or two of college or normal school, were recent graduates of the same schools. Because books were expensive, students learned mainly by rote and practiced writing on a slate. The elementary-school curriculum focused on the three R's, plus spelling and history.

New England was at the forefront of education in colonial America. Boston Latin School was founded in 1635, only five years after the town itself. A decade later, the Massachusetts Bay Colony required that every town of at least 50 families support a school and that all children be enrolled in it unless they were apprenticed to learn a trade. In the middle colonies, few schools were found outside towns and villages. In the South, education was reserved for propertied classes only. Plantation owners and well-off townsfolk employed private tutors for their sons and daughters.

Inside Old Sacramento Schoolhouse, Sacramento, California. Universal public education, perhaps more than any other factor, has helped create and maintain a great democracy. America's future rests in the minds and hearts of our children.

One-room schoolhouse, Coloma, California. Schoolhouses like this one once dotted the American landscape.

The ideal of universal education, so essential to American democracy, did not gain ground until public funding for schools began in the 1830s. Free and compulsory education had by then come to be viewed as the best way to Americanize and socialize the children of immigrants. Once again Massachusetts was the pioneer, establishing universal compulsory and free public education in 1852. It was 1918, however, before all states required children to attend elementary school.

Book-learning was not a survival skill on the colonial and early American frontier. Most children attended school spottily, if at all. Abraham Lincoln, encouraged by his stepmother, and Andrew Jackson, taught to read by his wife, are typical examples of frontier education in the 1820s and 1830s. As late as the mid-1880s, fewer than 60% of school-age children attended school in the Montana Territory. Nevertheless, from colonial times the United States had one of the highest literacy rates in the world. By 1840, 78% of the population and 91% of whites could read and write.

Even when schooling was required by law, it was a part-time affair that did not need a fancy building. Frontier settlers sited their schools in quickly erected log cabins or abandoned shacks and barns—sometimes as small as 10x12 feet, rarely containing more than one dimly lit room, inadequately heated by a wood- or coal-burning stove.

Originally most teachers were men. In the mid-18th century, when population growth and rapid territorial expansion created a shortage of qualified pedagogues, unmarried women were recruited to fill the gap. Parents and school committees could pay them lower salaries. Hundreds of women, attracted by the chance to escape farm-life drudgery and to pick a husband on the woman-starved frontier, left the East and Midwest to teach in frontier schools.

RULES FOR THE TEACHER

"Each day fill lamps, clean chimneys, bring a bucket of water and a scuttle of coal.

After 10 hours in school, you may spend the remaining time reading the Bible or other good books.

Men teachers may take one evening each week for courting purposes, or two evenings if they go to church regularly.

Women teachers who engage in unseemly conduct will be dismissed.

Once married, a woman must give up her teaching post to care for her family.

Any teacher who smokes, uses liquor, frequents pools or public halls, or gets shaved in a barber shop, will give good reason to suspect his worth, intention, integrity and honesty.

Make your pens carefully; you may whittle nibs to the individual taste for the pupils."

RULES FOR STUDENTS

"Before entering the classroom, form a line of boys and a line of girls. Girls will go in first.

Boys will sit on one side of the classroom and girls on the other.

Do not talk, smile, turn your head, or slouch when you are seated. Good posture is required. Talking is permitted during recess.

If you wish to speak, raise your hand and wait to be acknowledged. Do not speak unless spoken to.

If you are late, you will not be allowed inside the school.

Female students will conduct themselves as ladies, males as gentlemen."

—Old Sacramento Schoolhouse, Sacramento, California

ERIE CANAL
Hudson River & Great Lakes Link

FROM TROY, NEW YORK, TO BUFFALO, NEW YORK

Three Clintons have been prominent in American life: one was president, another vice-president (George Clinton, 1739–1812; governor of New York 1777–1795 and 1801–1804, vice-president 1805–1812). But the Clinton who did the most to shape America was in fact DeWitt Clinton (1769–1828), the far-seeing governor of New York (1817–1823 and 1825–1828) who was the father of the Erie Canal.

Today we take New York's position as the first city of the modern world for granted. In fact, during the first quarter of the 19th century it ranked behind Boston, Baltimore, Philadelphia, and New Orleans as a commercial port. Yet within 15 years after the opening of the canal it had overtaken all of them and was handling more cargo than Boston, Baltimore, and New Orleans combined. Meanwhile, the Great Lakes states (Ohio, Michigan, Illinois, Indiana, Wisconsin, and Minnesota), enjoying new markets, experienced phenomenal growth.

The seasonal navigability of canals and waterways, including those from Boston down to Charleston, was in part responsible for creating fall and spring markets for goods, such as clothing and books. Frozen waters in winter and insect life in the full heat of summer greatly restricted river and canal traffic in those seasons.

Waterford Flight is a series of locks on the Erie Canal in which boats are raised and lowered to the greatest heights in the shortest distance of any canal in the world.

Erie Canal Village, Rome, New York. This is a recreation of the 19th century community located at the site where, on July 4, 1817, the first shovelful of earth was turned for the construction of Erie Canal.

The 18th century had seen an explosion of canal-building in England and France. Water transport was the fastest, cheapest, highest-capacity, and most convenient method, far superior to horse-drawn conveyances traveling on rutted or muddy roads. The British colonies in North America, strung out along the seacoast, had little need for them, although a canal linking Lake Erie and the Hudson River was proposed as early as 1724. After independence, however, when the westward expansion into the Northwest Territory began, canal-building projects and companies sprang up in many places. Several studies were conducted to determine the best route for a canal between the Hudson River and the Great Lakes.

When the War of 1812 was over, DeWitt Clinton aligned himself at the head of the citizens of New York State who felt the time was ripe. Although opponents derided "Clinton's Folly," he persuaded the state legislature to appropriate funds for a canal between Troy and Buffalo. Work began on July 4, 1817. Its construction was an engineering feat of historic scale. Roads had to be built so that workers and supplies could reach excavation sites. Except for a few places where gunpowder was used to blast away rock, the entire canal—363 miles long, 40 feet wide, and 4 feet deep—was dug by the muscle power of men and animals.

After eight years of work, the Erie Canal was dedicated in a ceremony on October 26, 1825, when Clinton sailed from Buffalo at the head of a flotilla of three canal boats. Nine days later he arrived in Manhattan, to the acclaim of its citizens. Soon regular passenger service was established, reducing the transit time between New York and Buffalo from more than two weeks by stagecoach to about six days. Freight rates along the same route fell by 90%. In 1829, some 3,640 bushels of wheat were carried on the canal from Buffalo. By 1837, the amount was half a million, and four years later it was one million bushels.

Writing in 1816, Clinton foresaw the impact of his canal:

> "The most fertile and extensive regions of America will avail themselves of its facilities for a market. All their surplus productions...will concentrate in the city of New York, for transportation abroad or consumption at home....The city will, in the course of time, become the granary of the world, the emporium of commerce, the seat of manufactures, the focus of great moneyed operations and the concentrating point of vast disposable, and accumulating capital, which will stimulate, enliven, extend and reward the exertions of human labor and ingenuity.... Before the revolution of a century, the whole island of Manhattan, covered with inhabitants and replenished with a dense population, will constitute one vast city."

If only modern politicians were blessed with such prescience!

The Dismal Swamp Canal (1784), connecting the Chesapeake Bay in Virginia via the Elizabeth River and the Albemarle Sound in North Carolina via the Pasquotank River, is the oldest continually operating man-made canal in the United States. Today it is part of the Atlantic Intracoastal Waterway, which provides a protected channel for both pleasure boaters and ships between Norfolk, Virginia, and Miami, Florida.

The success of the Erie Canal led to the 19th century canal-building boom, which ended with the rise of railroads. Other canals, such as that between Philadelphia and Pittsburgh (1826–1834), enhanced commerce between cities. By 1850 more than 3,200 miles of canals had been dug in America.

WHITE HOUSE
1600 Pennsylvania Avenue

"You know that nobody is strong-minded around a President...it is always: 'yes, sir,' 'no, sir.'
(The 'no, sir' comes when he asks whether you're dissatisfied.)"—George Edward Reedy in R. Gordon Hoxie,
Ed., *The White House* (1971)

PRESIDENT'S PARK AND NATIONAL MALL, WASHINGTON, D.C.

No one attached much importance to the house occupied by Presidents Washington and Adams during the decade that Philadelphia was the temporary capital of the United States (1790–1800). In fact, the building was demolished in 1832 and its very location faded into the mists of historical confusion.

Not so when Washington and Pierre L'Enfant laid out the new Federal District on the banks of the Potomac. They chose a prominent elevation for a Presidential Palace that would be one of the major landmarks of the new city. Irish-born architect James Hoban won the design competition with a plan based on Leinster House in Dublin. The cornerstone laying, in October 1792, was the first for a public building in the new capital. By the autumn of 1800 it was deemed ready for occupancy; John Adams slept there for the first time on the night of November 1.

Sunset, White House, Washington, D.C.

White House, Washington, D.C.

When Thomas Jefferson (whose anonymous submission had lost to Hoban's) moved in four months later, he was less than enthusiastic about the amenities and design. He employed Benjamin Latrobe to modify and expand the building. After the British burned Washington in August 1814, leaving the Presidential Residence a gutted shell, President James Madison brought Hoban back to supervise its reconstruction. This, evidently, is when the gray stone exterior was first painted white (to hide the ravages of the fire).

The president's home remained largely unchanged, aside from the installation of modern utilities and conveniences, when the architect Latrobe rebuilt and enlarged the Capitol building. The first major renovation of the structure took place in 1902—a year after the popular name the "White House" was adopted officially—during Theodore Roosevelt's first term. Until then, the building had served both as a residence and as office space for the president and his handful of assistants (Lincoln, for example, with all his wartime cares, made do with two private secretaries). The "Executive Branch" meant the cabinet secretaries, who provided the president with whatever advice he required, and their departments. By Roosevelt's day, however, presidents were feeling the need for a larger staff loyal only to themselves. Hence the 1902 renovation included what, in retrospect, was the most significant new building in Washington since 1800—the West Wing, which provided office space for the president and an army of presidential staffers and gave the chief executive, for the first time, "troops" for contesting control of the government with the legislative branch. The Oval Office came to be identified as the seat of presidential power.

After World War II, the White House was in such poor physical condition that some proposed replacing it totally. But its image was too strongly entrenched for that. Instead, in a project that lasted from December 1948 to March 1952, the interior was gutted, leaving only the shell of the original exterior walls, and rebuilt to modern standards. (President Truman and his family relocated to Blair House, across the street.)

While the Capitol serves as the "theater of America," the White House has largely retained its private aspect. Presidents, alone with their families in the White House, had no audience to speak of. And Thomas Jefferson introduced a custom, which lasted for more than a century, that presidents did not go to Capitol Hill to address Congress in person. But the concentrated power of the executive, wielded from the White House, increasingly tended to overshadow the legislature. By the time Congress began televising its proceedings, chief executives speaking from the Oval Office had usurped its role as the leading thespians of American politics.

"I pray Heaven to bestow the Best of Blessings on this House and all that shall hereafter inhabit it. May none but honest and wise Men ever rule under this roof."—John Adams to Abigail Adams, November 2, 1800

THE CAPITOL

The House & the Senate, the Voices of America

CAPITOL HILL, WASHINGTON, D.C.

In Philadelphia, Congress met in what had been built to serve as the County Courthouse, adjacent to the state-house (Independence Hall). President George Washington and Pierre L'Enfant selected Jenkins' Hill, the highest eminence in the new Federal District, as the site of the permanent home for Congress, which soon earned the designation "Capitol." The name derives from the classical Latin term for a hilltop citadel or temple: the Founders perceived the seat of the legislature precisely as a citadel or temple of liberty. The architectural competition for the Capitol was won by an amateur, Dr. William Thornton. His design called for a sandstone building with two wings flanking a central hall with a shallow-domed rotunda. Washington laid the cornerstone in September 1793, but progress on this much larger edifice was slow. When the government moved to Washington City in 1800, only the north (Senate) wing was ready.

Benjamin Latrobe took over direction of the Capitol project, and by 1807, the House wing was usable (it was completed in 1811) and the Senate wing, which had been poorly executed, was about to undergo its first renovation. Only an open wooden portico connected the two chambers.

After the British, in the War of 1812, set the Capitol and other Washington buildings on fire in 1814, Latrobe modified his design again as reconstruction proceeded. In 1826 architect Charles Bulfinch completed the Capitol, more or less in keeping with Latrobe's plan, including a copper-covered wooden dome over the central section.

Sunset, Capitol Hill, Washington, D.C.

Capitol Hill, Washington, D.C.

As new states were admitted and the country grew, so did the number of senators and representatives. Congress quickly felt cramped in its home. Within two decades it proved necessary to erect what was essentially a new structure. Architect Thomas Walter added marble-faced Greek Revival wings for the two houses, more than doubling the length of the building; their interiors were completed by 1859 (the exterior took another decade). The old dome was replaced by a 270-foot cast-iron dome, topped by Thomas Crawford's 19½-foot bronze statue of "Armed Freedom." Work on the new dome continued even after the Civil War began and was completed with the installation of the statue in December 1863.

The need for more office space inspired a 32½-foot extension of the east front in 1958–1962; the new marble façade was constructed to replicate the original sandstone façade.

The public nature of the Capitol is reflected in the fact that it has always served as the "theater of America." (The White House, in contrast, has a private aspect.) Especially during the four decades before the Civil War, when the country was struggling to fashion its identity and the Senate included men like Henry Clay, John C. Calhoun, Daniel Webster, Thomas Hart Benton, Sam Houston, Lewis Cass, William Seward, Salmon P. Chase, Jefferson Davis, and Stephen Douglas, Congressional debates riveted the attention of Americans. Oratory—carefully structured speeches that made their logical points one by one over a period of several hours (Daniel Webster's famous "Seventh of March" speech, in support of the Compromise of 1850, lasted more than three hours)—was still a highly appreciated art; the newspapers reprinted and schoolboys committed to memory the most famous speeches of the day.

In the mid-20th century, when radio and then television were admitted to congressional committee rooms, the major dramas took place there—notably the Army-McCarthy hearings of the early 1950s and the Ervine and Rodino committees of the Watergate era. In the last few decades, the dynamics of visible power have changed, with more attention given to the White House and Presidential speeches broadcast from the Oval Office than to debates in the House and Senate.

AFRICAN MEETING HOUSE
African-American Churches & Early Abolitionists

BEACON HILL, BOSTON, MASSACHUSETTS

In 1787, the white elders of St. George's Methodist Church in Philadelphia ordered black worshippers, formerly accommodated on the main floor, to sit in a newly built gallery. Several free blacks refused, including former slave Richard Allen. He proceeded to establish the Free African Society of Philadelphia and, seven years later, a separate black church—the first in the United States.

Even in Massachusetts, where slavery had been declared unconstitutional in 1781, African-Americans did not enjoy any semblance of social equality. Boston blacks, who were not legally barred from white schools, actually set up their own segregated schools around 1800, seeking to improve their children's education. A similar process of self-segregation took place in religious life.

Although no church in Boston excluded African-Americans, they were not accepted as voting members of the congregation (and New England churches were run by their members, not by their preachers or a church hierarchy) and were frequently relegated to the balcony.

Façade of the African Meeting House, Boston, Massachusetts. Early abolitionists met here.

Church in the African Meeting House, Boston, Massachusetts. In churches across America, African-Americans planted the seeds and nurtured the hopes for both the abolition of slavery and for the later Civil Rights Movement. Today these churches form the heart of many African-American communities and continue to be the fertile ground upon which social and intellectual growth flourishes. In the mid-20th century, more and more white congregations began to welcome people of color to worship beside them.

New England clergymen were members of the educated elite; Harvard and Yale were founded explicitly to teach theology and train young men for the ministry. Black preachers, by contrast, achieved their status through charisma; since this was no qualification in the major white denominations, most black congregations were Baptist or Methodist. These evangelical denominations had a further attraction for blacks. In the austere rite of Puritan churches, singing and emotion were almost mortal sins. For African-Americans, they were the natural way to pray, reminiscent of their still-remembered tribal traditions.

Hence blacks tried to find other venues for worship, but ran into the problem of raising money to build their own churches. In 1805, the black preacher Thomas Paul, whose congregation had been meeting at Faneuil Hall, gathered 20 parishioners and organized the First African Baptist Church. With funds collected from both blacks and sympathetic whites, a plot of land was purchased and a building constructed. The new African Meeting House—the oldest surviving black church in the United States—was dedicated in December 1806. (Even at that ceremony, however, the members of the congregation were seated in the balcony, while white patrons and sympathizers were ushered to the pews on the main floor.)

Within a decade, separate black Baptist, Methodist, and Presbyterian churches had been established in Philadelphia, Boston, New York, and Wilmington, Delaware. In 1816, Richard Allen founded the first autonomous black denomination, the African Methodist Episcopal Church. The rival African Methodist Episcopal Zion Church was established in New York five years later.

In addition to its primary use as a church, the African Meeting House also served as a schoolhouse for black children and as the main forum of the African-American community in Boston. It was often referred to as the "black Faneuil Hall." It was here, for example, that William Lloyd Garrison founded the New England Anti-Slavery Society in 1832.

Churches remain the heart and mind of African-American communities across the nation. Out of them came resistance to Jim Crow laws and segregation, leaders in the Civil Rights Movement, and the impetus for important social, cultural, educational, and political advances.

When the black community moved away from the north slope of Beacon Hill in the late 19th century, the Meeting House was sold to a Jewish congregation. It served as a synagogue until the Museum of Afro-American History purchased it in 1972.

HANCOCK SHAKER VILLAGE
Utopias, Social Reform & Religious Radicalism

"Unto you, O, men, I call; and my voice is to the sons of man. Hear, for I will speak of excellent things, and the opening of my lips shall be right things."—The Divine Book of Holy & Eternal Wisdom

NEW HARMONY, INDIANA; ECONOMY, PENNSYLVANIA; BROOK FARM, AND PITTSFIELD, MASSACHUSETTS; AND SOCIETIES ACROSS AMERICA

Early 19th century society held an optimistic faith in human perfectibility. Americans attempted social experiments and reform programs designed to emancipate the human spirit, improve social conditions, and revolutionize economic organization. Among the great humanitarian reformers were also members of utopian communities and radical religious sects.

Robert Owen, an English philanthropist, founded a utopian community in New Harmony, Indiana, in 1824; his community became a model for other would-be utopias. (After Owen's arrival, George Rapp's

Round Stone Barn, Hancock Shaker Village, Pittsfield, Massachusetts. The Shakers excelled in craftsmanship. Their simple and functional designs in furniture and other goods have been widely copied. They display both beauty (though not necessarily intended) and economy in design. This round barn maximizes efficiency.

Harmony Society moved to Economy, Pennsylvania, and survived until 1903.) New Harmony attracted noted scientists, educators, and writers, but the economic and educational system was radical on religion and marriage, which limited its long-term possibilities. The community reportedly had the first kindergarten, free public school, free library, and school with equal education for boys and girls. (These first things are a matter of debate.)

Albert Brisbane, who advocated organizing society into phalanxes of less than 1,800 people who cooperated in science, industry, and art, popularized Frenchman Charles Fourier's philosophic principles. About 30 such phalanxes were established in the U.S.; the most famous was Brook Farm, founded by New England transcendentalists, such as Nathaniel Hawthorne and Sophia Dana Ripley.

Etienne Cabet proposed communistic Icarian communities, tested in a Texas colony on the Red River, which moved to Illinois in 1849. Communities in Missouri, Iowa, and California followed their example.

Religious communities, some dating from previous centuries, took radical or fantastic forms. Among them were the Pietists (1694) and Dunkers (1732) in Pennsylvania, the Shakers in Watervliet, New York (1776), the Separatists (1817), and the Amana Society (1859). In Oneida, New York, John Humphrey formed the Perfectionists, who practiced polygamy and engaged in religious and social experiments in communal living. The society survived about 30 years, until 1881. William Miller preached of the immediate second coming of Christ, and Millerites prepared for the end of the world, expected in 1844. Other mid-19th century social reform movements were inspired by the belief that Americans were rapidly approaching the ideal of a perfect society.

Humanitarian reformers worked to aid disabled people, revised the penal system, fought for temperance, and campaigned for women's rights and universal education. Thomas H. Gallaudet established a Hartford,

Connecticut, school for the deaf (1816). Other achievements were the Perkins Institute for the Education of the Blind (1829) and a Worcester, Massachusetts, state asylum for the mentally ill (1833). Dorthea Dix helped revolutionize care and treatment of people with mental illness and mental retardation. Inhumane punishment and imprisonment for debt were abolished. Decent workhouses were created. Benjamin Rush and Lyman Beecher formed in Boston the American Temperance Society in 1821 and urged thousands to sign a temperance pledge. Legislation, such as the Maine law of 1851, forbade the manufacturing, importing, and selling of intoxicating beverages.

Tan House, Hancock Shaker Village, Pittsfield, Massachusetts. Built in 1835, originally a leather tannery, the building was adapted in 1875 for cider pressing, blacksmithing, woodworking, and milling.

ALAMO
Mexican War & Texas Independence

"I am determined to sustain myself as long as possible and die like a soldier who never forgets what is due to his own honor and that of his country: VICTORY OR DEATH."—Lt. Col. William Barret Travis, February 24, 1836

SAN ANTONIO, TEXAS

The 18-minute battle of San Jacinto (April 21, 1836) was far more important than its size—fewer than 3,000 combatants—would indicate. When the Texas army, under Sam Houston, routed the Mexican forces under Santa Anna it ensured the independence of the Lone Star Republic. Nine years later the United States annexed Texas. This in turn sparked the Mexican War, which transferred California and the Southwest to the United States. The vast new acquisition exacerbated the debate about slavery and popular sovereignty and set the country on the road to the Civil War.

The Alamo, San Antonio, Texas, Mission San Antonio de Valero, was one of several early 17th century missions. When missionary activity waned, the compound was abandoned in 1793. After 1803, when soldiers dispatched from a base at Alamo de Parras converted the empty building into a barracks, the compound was known as the Alamo, *"cottonwood" in Spanish.*

At the end of Mexico's war of independence, in 1821, its most northeastern district, Texas, had three towns and a population of 2,500. Within 13 years, immigration from the United States had created an Anglo population of some 20,000.

The Mexican federal constitution of 1824, which established a division of powers between the central government and the states, appealed to the Anglos. The federal authorities encouraged their immigration as the best way to develop the area and allowed the states to regulate it as they saw fit. The leaders of Coahuila state, which included Texas, did everything they could to accommodate the immigrants, who could provide security from Indians, develop agriculture, and expand commercial ties with the United States.

The Alamo, San Antonio, Texas.

Mexican law limited immigration to Catholics, but the immigrants, even if they went through a form of conversion, continued to practice their Protestantism. After 1831 slavery was illegal in Mexico, but the immigrants continued to hold slaves to work their cotton and sugar plantations. And, of course, they spoke a different language.

These and other problems might have been worked out, though, were it not for the Mexican political contest between the Centralists, who advocated an autocratic and centralized regime, and the Federalists. A year after the Centralists gained power in 1829, they passed a law banning Anglo immigration. The Texas Anglos (or "Texians") rallied to the Federalist cause.

The six flags of Texas are the Spanish (1519–1685, 1690–1821), French (1685–1690), Mexican (1821–1836), Republic of Texas (1836–1845), Confederacy (1861–1865), and American (1845–1861, 1865–present). The Lone Star, today the state flag, also flew over the Republic of Texas.

In 1833, Gen. Antonio López de Santa Anna seized power in Mexico City as a Federalist, but soon deserted to the Centralist camp. He abrogated the Constitution of 1824 and replaced the federal states with departments governed by presidential appointees. The Federalists in Coahuila raised militia units and demanded the restoration of the Constitution of 1824. The Mexican commander in San Antonio appealed for reinforcements. To intercept them, a force commanded by 26-year-old William Travis captured the military post at Anáhuac, about forty miles southwest of Laredo, in June 1835. Following the Battle of Gonzales, in October, Texian volunteers laid siege to San Antonio, which they captured on December 10.

Most of the Texian militia went back home after the capture of San Antonio, leaving behind a small garrison, consisting mainly of volunteers recently arrived from the United States.

On February 23, Santa Anna and his forces arrived unexpectedly outside San Antonio. Travis, in command there, withdrew his men into an old Spanish mission (converted into an army barracks in 1803) now equipped with palisades and cannon.

Travis's pleas for help, issued "in the name of Liberty, of patriotism and everything dear to the American[!] character," brought him only 32 volunteer reinforcements; his total strength was probably less than 190 men. Santa Anna had 5,000 soldiers. After a 12-day siege, the Mexicans launched an all-out assault at daybreak on March 6. Within three hours, all the defenders were dead. The defenders never knew that four days earlier the Texian council, meeting in Austin, had voted for independence.

The news of the Alamo's fall set off a mass flight of Anglo settlers. But it also put an end to squabbling among the revolutionary leaders and enabled Sam Houston to organize and train the Texian forces, who took the bravery of the defenders of San Antonio to heart. When his troops charged the enemy on that fateful day at San Jacinto, their battle cry was "Remember the Alamo!"

SUTTER'S MILL

Gold Rush, California Glitter & Ghost Towns

"Men rush to California and Australia as if the true gold were to be found in that direction; but that is to go to the very opposite extreme to where it lies..."—Henry David Thoreau, *Life without Principle* (1863)

COLOMA, CALIFORNIA, AND THE SIERRA NEVADA FOOTHILLS

When Johann Sutter, fleeing creditors in his native Switzerland and at earlier stops in North America, arrived in California in 1839, it was a distant and sparsely populated province of Mexico. Obtaining a grant of 48,000 acres in what is now the Sacramento Valley, he founded the model agricultural colony he called New Helvetia. It soon became a magnet for the trickle of immigrants from the United States and played a role in their uprising against the Mexican authorities that dovetailed into the Mexican War of 1846–1848. When that war was ended by the Treaty of Guadalupe Hidalgo, California's non-Indian population was less than 15,000.

In January 1848, James Marshall, who was constructing a sawmill for Sutter at what is now Coloma on the American River, in the foothills of the Sierra Nevada, spotted two small nuggets in the millrace. In this case, what glittered *was* gold, as Marshall surmised and Sutter himself proved several days later. The two agreed to

John Sutter's Sawmill, Coloma, California. The original mill closed in 1850; this is an exact replica built in 1967 based on James Marshall's own drawings.

keep their find a secret until the mill was finished. But their workers knew and Sutter himself may not have been as discreet as he should. The news soon leaked out. Because there had been at least one previous abortive discovery of gold in California, most people were initially skeptical about the report, even after a San Francisco paper publicized it in March.

Two months later, in mid-May, Sam Brannan, a Mormon elder who lived in San Francisco, verified the report when he obtained gold dust as a church tithe from workers at Sutter's Mill. Back home, Brannan first bought up all the mining tools in town and then took to the streets with his precious evidence. Seeing is believing, and Brannan was able to resell at $15 apiece, the tin pans he had bought in the morning for 20 cents. (He made $36,000 over the next two months.) Within three days, some 200 of the town's male residents had left to pan for gold, including 34 deserters from the 50-man U.S. Army garrison. Sailors jumped ship, farmers abandoned their plows; even the San Francisco newspapers had to suspend publication for lack of pressmen. The mania was understandable. A laborer earned a dollar a day—but an ounce of gold sold for $16, and if you found a rich claim you could dig up ten ounces in a day.

Communications with the Atlantic coast, overland or by sea, were excruciatingly slow. It was only in the second half of August that the New York *Herald* carried the first report of the strike. After President James K. Polk confirmed it in his December message to Congress, the Gold Rush was on. The non-Native population of California, 20,000 at the end of 1848, was 100,000 a year later and 250,000 by the end of 1852.

"Sutter's Mill" marking the location on the bank of the American River where, in January 1848, James Marshall picked up the the small pieces of gold that touched off one of the largest mass migrations in history.

These heavy-loaded wagons supplied gold-mine camps throughout the Sierra Nevada from the mid-1850s through the early 20th century. Eight to 20 mules or horses pulled the two-wagon rig. Mounted on the wheel-horse, the teamster used a single "jerk line" along the line to control the team. Jerk Line Freight Outfit, Marshall Gold Discovery State Historical Park, Coloma, California.

Because the trip to California was long and arduous, the Forty-Niners were mainly middle-class Americans who could finance the adventure. Most of them lacked the physical stamina and ruthlessness required to succeed as gold miners. A few did parlay their digging into lasting wealth. In general, however, it was the merchants and artisans who satisfied the needs of the exploding population—such as storekeeper Leland Stanford and tailor Levi Strauss—who made their fortunes in California. (Brannan, for example, became California's first millionaire before drinking away his money.)

Its population bolstered by the Gold Rush, California was admitted to the Union in 1850. The addition of a state on the Pacific coast changed the political geography of the country. The delicate equilibrium between North and South, free states and slave, which had been the key to American politics for the last three decades, was irreparably breached. Marshall, Sutter, Brannan, and the Forty-Niners, pursuing their own private visions, unwittingly set off a chaotic madness that, ironically, eventually realized the dream of "one nation indivisible."

SENECA FALLS
Women's Suffrage & Rights Slowly Won

"We hold these truths to be self-evident: that all men and women are created equal; that they are endowed by their Creator with certain inalienable rights; that among these are life, liberty, and the pursuit of happiness; that to secure these rights governments are instituted, deriving their just powers from the consent of the governed. Whenever any form of government becomes destructive of these ends, it is the right of those who suffer from it to refuse allegiance to it, and to insist upon the institution of a new government, laying its foundation on such principles, and organizing its powers in such form, as to them shall seem most likely to effect their safety and happiness..."—Elizabeth Cady Stanton, "The Declaration of Sentiments" (1848)

SENECA FALLS, NEW YORK

In the early 19th century, both sexes believed that women were delicate creatures, physically and morally. Law or custom barred them from voting, speaking in public, holding office, obtaining higher education, or working outside the home except as teachers, seamstresses, domestic servants, or mill workers. Married women could not conclude contracts, file lawsuits, initiate divorce on grounds other than adultery, or own property. These restrictions were intended to protect them from being sullied by the rough-and-tumble of business and politics. By radiating their superior moral sense in the home, however, they could have a positive influence on their menfolk and thus on society as a whole.

Remains of the Wesleyan Chapel, site of the First Women's Rights Convention.

Starting in the 1830s, American women began trying to exercise this beneficent influence in the public sphere as well, on behalf of causes such as health reform, temperance, the reform of prostitutes and public morality, and especially abolition.

Criticism of their unprecedented intrusion into "men's affairs" soon led women in the antislavery movement to note the similarity between women and blacks. In the words of Lydia Maria Child, "both have been kept in subjection by physical force and considered rather in the light of property than as individuals."

In 1840, after the World Anti-Slavery Convention in London excluded the American women delegates, two of them, Elizabeth Cady Stanton and Lucretia Mott, decided to convene a women's rights convention when they returned home. Eight years passed before it finally met, at the Wesleyan Methodist Chapel near their Seneca Falls, New York, homes, on July 19–20, 1848.

The centerpiece of the convention was the "Declaration of Sentiments," a pastiche of the Declaration of Independence: "We hold these truths to be self-evident; that all men *and women* are created equal." It protested the lack of educational and professional opportunities for women and railed against laws that assumed male superiority and gave men all power in matters of property, divorce, and child custody.

DECLARATION OF SENTIMENTS

When, in the course of human events,
it becomes necessary for one portion of the family of man
to assume among the people of the earth
a position different from that which they have hitherto occupied,
but one to which the laws of nature
and of nature's God entitle them,
a decent respect to the opinions of mankind requires
that they should declare the causes
that impel them to such a course.

We hold these truths to be self-evident:
that all men and women are created equal;
that they are endowed by their Creator
with certain inalienable rights;
that among these are life, liberty, and the pursuit of happiness;
that to secure these rights governments are instituted,
deriving their just powers from the consent of the governed—
Whenever any form of Government
becomes destructive of these ends,
it is the right of those who suffer from it to refuse allegiance to it,

Declaration Park features a granite wall engraved with the "Declaration of Sentiments" and the names of the women who signed it.

The delegates decried the existence of different moral codes for men and women. In brief, they protested the fact that man "has endeavored, in every way that he could, to destroy [woman's] confidence in her own powers, to lessen her self-respect, and to make her willing to lead a dependent and abject life." The only resolution that provoked debate and was not approved unanimously was Stanton's call for a struggle to achieve women's "inalienable right to the elective franchise."

Despite the opposition at Seneca Falls, the demand for suffrage soon became the core of the feminist struggle, replacing the earlier campaign to right a broad spectrum of socioeconomic wrongs. The leading advocate of this single-minded approach was Susan B. Anthony, who first met Stanton in 1851.

For the next half-century Stanton and Anthony worked together. Stanton the ideologue who saw the women's movement as a whole; Anthony the doer who devised and implemented vocal strategies and tactics aimed at winning the vote as the key to full equality.

It was a long and arduous campaign. The post–Civil War constitutional amendments that granted rights to the freed slaves also entrenched women's political disability. The first openings appeared in 1869 and 1870, when the Wyoming and Utah territories gave women the vote. Wyoming, admitted to the Union in 1890, was the first state with female suffrage. Over the next three decades the suffragettes intensified their crusade. In 1918, Jeannette Rankin of Montana, the first woman elected to Congress, introduced a constitutional amendment to enfranchise women. It was ratified in 1920.

Anthony had won her struggle, though posthumously, and eventually found her place in the ultimate pantheon of the United States—its coinage. The specific complaints of the Seneca Falls program have been remedied. The failure of the Equal Rights Amendment to win ratification in the 1980s suggests, however, that Anthony was naive: voting is not enough to achieve full equality.

PONY EXPRESS OFFICES
Relay Postal Service in Rain, Sleet, Snow & Rocky Mountain Gale

"I do hereby swear, before the Great and Living God, that during my engagement, and while I am an employee of Russell, Majors & Waddell, that I will, under no circumstances, use profane language; that I will drink no intoxicating liquors; that I will not quarrel or fight with any other employee of the firm, and that in every respect I will conduct myself honestly, be faithful to my duties, and so direct all my acts as to win the confidence of my employers. So help me God."—Pony Express riders' pledge for Central Overland California and Pikes Peak Express Company

TRAILS FROM MISSOURI AND KANSAS THROUGH COLORADO, WYOMING, UTAH, NEVADA, TO CALIFORNIA

In 1847, when California and the Southwest passed under U.S. control, Congress authorized postal service to the Pacific Coast. Heavily subsidized private contractors carried the mail. One of them, the Overland Mail Company ("Butterfield Express"), ran stagecoaches between Fort Smith, Arkansas, and San Francisco, via Texas and the Arizona Territory; the one-way trip took three to four weeks.

In early 1860, hoping to land a Federal mail contract to California, the Central Overland California and Pikes Peak Express Company, which already provided freight and stagecoach connections between the Missouri River and Salt Lake City, promised to establish a new express system within two months. Borrowing an idea at least as old as the Persian Empire, it established relay stations, recruited riders, and purchased horses. On April 3, 1860, the first Pony Express rider left the railhead at St. Joseph, Missouri, with 49 letters. Another rider left Sacramento, headed east, on April 4.

Sand Springs Pony Express Station, Nevada. Located at the base of Sand Mountain, Nevada, Sand Springs is a perfect example of the isolation and living conditions at a Pony Express station. Sir Richard Burton, the British explorer who visited the Sand Springs Pony Express Station, wrote: "The station house was…roofless and chairless, filthy and squalid, with smoky fire in one corner, and a table in the center of an impure floor….The walls open to every wind and interior full of dust…."

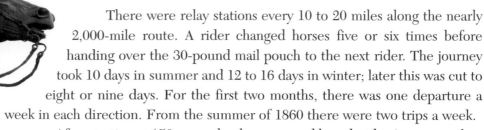

There were relay stations every 10 to 20 miles along the nearly 2,000-mile route. A rider changed horses five or six times before handing over the 30-pound mail pouch to the next rider. The journey took 10 days in summer and 12 to 16 days in winter; later this was cut to eight or nine days. For the first two months, there was one departure a week in each direction. From the summer of 1860 there were two trips a week.

After starting at $50 a month, plus room and board, riders' average salary rose to $100 to $125, and up to $150 a month for the most hazardous stretches—not bad, considering that the CEO of the entire operation was paid $250 to $300 a month and that regional managers got $90 a month. Hostile natives killed one rider and at least one station manager.

Initially the Pony Express charged $5 per half-ounce. By the end of the service the operators, trying to keep the *mochilla,* or mail pouch, full, had lowered the rate to $1 per half-ounce.

As a public-relations exercise, the Pony Express made special efforts to get important political news to the West Coast in record time. It carried the results of the presidential election of 1860 from Ft. Kearney, Nebraska Territory (the western terminus of the telegraph, about 100 miles west of St. Joseph) to Fort Churchill, Nevada (the eastern end of the California telegraph) in a week. (Thus, the Pony Express filled in where the telegraph could not.) Californians knew the results of the November 6 election

Pony Express Statue, Sacramento, California. Here the Pony Express started on April 4, 1860, when Sam Hamilton galloped into a blinding rainstorm on the first lap of the 1,966 mile trip to St. Joseph, Missouri.

by November 14. Four months later, extra horses and riders were put on to speed the text of Lincoln's inaugural address—the first public statement of his attitude toward the secession crisis—westward; it reached California in seven days and 17 hours (plus a few milliseconds on the telegraph line). Californians knew about the bombardment of Fort Sumter within nine days.

It was clear from the outset that the Pony Express was a stopgap, soon to be made obsolete by the telegraph and railroad. On October 26, 1861, two days after the two halves of the transcontinental telegraph line met in Salt Lake City, the Pony Express officially suspended operations. It had proven a financial disaster, losing its owners at least $200,000. But during the crucial months before and after the start of the Civil War, it was California's umbilical cord to the rest of the country and merits some of the credit for keeping that state in the Union. Meanwhile, the solitary bravery of its young riders captured the hearts and the imagination of the American people.

U.S. Postal Service take note: in its 18 months of operation the Pony Express lost only one mail pouch.

MAIL-ORDER CATALOGS

Since colonial times, people have bought goods by mail. While farmers and frontier people's outhouse uses for the Ward and Sears catalog pages may amuse us, these catalogs made a big difference in their lives. The growth of mail-order houses in the 1870s and 1880s, free rural delivery in the 1890s, and parcel post in 1913 meant that isolated American farmers could have access to good-quality merchandise at reasonable prices. Local merchants in nearby towns offered only a limited number of goods sold at relatively high prices. With mail order, customers in the most remote parts of America could order a cook stove, sewing machine, hammer, wagon, plow, or clothing and have these items delivered to their door. By 1900, the Chicago-based Sears, Roebuck & Company annually sold more than $10 million in mail-order merchandise.

LEWIS & HARRIET HAYDEN HOUSE
Underground Railroad "Station"

"I was the conductor of the Underground Railroad for eight years, and I can say what most conductors can't say—I never ran my train off the track and I never lost a passenger."—Harriet Tubman (1821–1913), former African-American slave and liberator of slaves

BOSTON, MASSACHUSETTS

The first blacks brought to Virginia, in 1619, were free, though indentured, whereas the first Africans carried to Massachusetts, in 1638, were slaves. Three years later, Massachusetts Bay and Plymouth were the first North American colonies to grant legal recognition to slavery; it was 1660 before Virginia did the same. Crispus Attucks, the mulatto who instigated and was killed in the Boston Massacre (1770), had spent the first 27 years of his life as the slave of a Massachusetts master. Significantly, however, after escaping in 1750 he managed to evade recapture and live as a free man for two decades.

The Lewis and Harriet Hayden House, Boston, Massachusetts. In 1849 escaped slave Lewis Hayden and his wife Harriet moved into this house and allowed their home to become a "station" on the Underground Railroad. In the mid-1800s, many such sites dotted the United States.

HOME OF **LEWIS HAYDEN** 1811-1889

FUGITIVE SLAVE - LEADING ABOLITIONIST
PRINCE HALL MASON - RESCUER OF SHADRACH
MEMBER OF THE GENERAL COURT
MESSENGER TO THE SECRETARY OF THE STATE

A MEETING PLACE OF ABOLITIONISTS
AND A STATION ON
THE UNDERGROUND RAILROAD
THE HERITAGE GUILD, INC.

*Plaque on the Lewis and Harriet House,
Boston, Massachusetts.*

For although Massachusetts lacked the Quaker heritage of Pennsylvania, the passion for freedom that made it the cradle of the American Revolution soon made it feel uncomfortable with black slavery. The Declaration of Rights appended to its constitution in 1780 declared, "All men are born free and equal." The next year, the courts freed a slave named Quork Walker, on the grounds that slavery was now unconstitutional in the commonwealth. (Most other northern states passed legislation abolishing or setting a term to involuntary servitude for those unborn, but emancipated current slaves only gradually or not at all.) At the time of the first U.S. census in 1790, Massachusetts was the only state that reported no slaves among its population. A decade later, the 1,100 African-Americans in Boston constituted one of the largest communities of free blacks in the country.

It was only natural that Boston became the center of the abolitionist movement, which sought to outlaw the immoral practice of chattel bondage throughout the country, and of the Underground Railroad, which had the more immediate objective of rescuing slaves from their evil condition. In 1793, Congress passed a fugitive slave law, empowering slave owners to recover their "property" even if "it" had fled to a free state. But in the northern states this was felt to be a disgraceful law; some, like Massachusetts, actually passed legislation making it illegal to comply with the national law. As early as 1818, loosely organized networks, largely white, helped slaves escape to free states or, for total security, to Canada. This arrangement came to be known as the "Underground Railroad."

The activity of the Underground Railroad accelerated after the U.S. Supreme Court ruled in 1842 that state officials did not have to help return fugitive slaves to their masters. This outraged the South; hence one of the elements of Henry Clay's Compromise of 1850 was an enforceable national Fugitive Slave Act. After its passage—and even more so after the Supreme Court's Dred Scott decision in 1857, which held that African-Americans could not even be U.S. citizens—no place in the North was a truly safe haven for runaway slaves. This situation exacerbated abolitionist sentiment in the North. Other elements of the Compromise may have postponed the Civil War, but the Fugitive Slave Act made it inevitable.

Most of the buildings that were way stations on the Underground Railroad, as well as most of its agents and "conductors," were better served by anonymity and have been forgotten today. A salient exception is the Boston home of Lewis Hayden (spirited out of his master's house in Lexington, Kentucky, by a Vermont abolitionist) and his wife Harriet. According to legend, the Haydens kept two kegs of gunpowder under their front stoop. Whenever bounty hunters or process servers showed up in search of runaway slaves, the Haydens came out bearing lighted candles, which they threatened to drop and blow up the house rather than surrender the human beings who had found shelter with them.

"The only free road, the Underground Railroad, is owned and managed by the Vigilant Committee. They have tunneled under the whole breadth of the land."—Henry David Thoreau (1817–1862)

FORT SUMTER
First Shot of the Civil War

The surrender of Fort Sumter was "virtually a surrender of the Union."—Francis P. Blair, April 12, 1861

CHARLESTON HARBOR, SOUTH CAROLINA

At the end of the Polk administration, in 1849, the United States seemed poised for greatness. Under his stewardship, Texas had been annexed, the Southwest and California wrested from Mexico, and a compromise achieved with Britain on the Pacific Northwest. The dream of Manifest Destiny had been realized: the country now spanned the continent. But within 12 years it would be split asunder by a bloody civil war.

The problem was slavery. Some Northerners viewed it as a moral evil that must be eradicated from the entire country. Most were willing to accept it where it already existed but opposed its extension to the new territories. Southerners were adamantly against any limitations on their "peculiar institution."

The issue came to a head with California's application for statehood in 1850. Henry Clay of Kentucky authored his last great compromise and the crisis was deferred. When it resurfaced in 1854, the Kansas-Nebraska Act bought off the South for a few more years.

The Whig party crumbled under the strain. By 1860 the Democrats, too, could no longer sit together. The party convention adjourned after delegates from the Deep South walked out to protest its refusal to endorse

Fort Sumter, on Charleston Bay, South Carolina. When the Civil War ended, Fort Sumter bore little resemblance to the impressive work that stood there when the war began in 1861. Fort Sumter today bears only a superficial similarity to its original appearance.

Flags of the Fort: The flags flying from the five shorter flag-poles that surround the American flag represent the flags flown over Fort Sumter during the Civil War.

slavery in the territories. Two months later, at separate conventions, one wing nominated Stephen Douglas of Illinois; the other, John C. Breckinridge of Kentucky. Remnants of the Whigs, organized as the Constitutional Union Party, nominated John Bell of Tennessee. All three platforms were "soft" on slavery. The six-year-old Republican Party nominated Abraham Lincoln of Illinois on a platform that rejected any extension of slavery.

All presidents except for the two Adamses had been slaveholders or sympathetic to the South. So panic gripped the South when, in what was really two sectional elections—Lincoln vs. Douglas in the North, Breckinridge vs. Bell in the South—Lincoln swept the North and won.

The Deep South did not wait to see what he would do in office. Beginning with South Carolina, on December 20, seven states seceded from the Union. In February 1861 they established the Confederate States of America.

Meanwhile, unionists tried to fashion another compromise, including a constitutional amendment barring congressional interference with slavery. Lincoln maintained a public silence. Privately, he let it be known that he would support an amendment protecting slavery in its current limits but opposed measures to extend slavery in the territories.

In his inaugural address (March 4), Lincoln stated that secession was legally void and the secessionists were rebels. Nevertheless, he would not use force against the secessionists. But he would defend U.S. property.

All eyes turned to two Federal installations in the South that had not yet been seized by state militias—Ft. Pickens in Pensacola, Florida, and Ft. Sumter in Charleston Harbor.

Lincoln was in a quandary. Abandoning the forts would offend many Republicans and bolster the secessionists' international legitimacy. Forcibly resupplying and reinforcing their garrisons would alienate the Upper South. Finally he decided to reinforce Pickens but only resupply the more visible Sumter.

On April 10 the Confederate government instructed Gen. P. G. T. Beauregard to fire on Sumter to prevent its resupply or reinforcement. The next day Beauregard called on its commander, Maj. Robert Anderson, to surrender. Anderson declined, but added that he would run out of food by the 15th and have to abandon the fort unless resupplied.

The secessionists could not wait. The bombardment began at 4:30 A.M. on April 12. Anderson and his men hunkered down for 34 hours. Then, with the walls and main gates seriously damaged and flames threatening the magazines, he surrendered. On April 14 Anderson and his men marched out of Sumter and took ship for New York.

Lincoln issued an immediate call for volunteers to put down the rebellion. Four border states responded by casting their lot with the Confederacy. The battle lines were drawn. Almost everyone, North and South, thought the war would be over by mid-summer. They were wrong.

GETTYSBURG

Union & Confederate Bloodshed, 50,000 Casualties

GETTYSBURG, PENNSYLVANIA

We all remember Clark Gable telling off a room full of Southern bloods eager to go out and whip the Yankees, reciting statistics that proved the South couldn't possibly defeat the Union. But that is movie history, 20/20 hindsight. To put down the rebellion, the North had to defeat the rebel armies and occupy almost the entire territory of the Confederacy. The South only had to make the North decide that the cost of preserving the Union was too steep. Thus on the first three days of July 1863, even though Union armies occupied large swaths of Confederate territory and at Vicksburg Grant was poised to cut the Confederacy in two, the outcome of the war hung in the balance at Gettysburg.

The Confederates had followed up their victory at Chancellorsville in early May by invading Pennsylvania, hoping to relieve the pressure on Richmond, the Confederate capital, and outflank Washington. Southern politicians believed that the fall or investment of the northern capital would spur England and France to recognize the Confederacy and force the Union to accept secession. At Gettysburg, some 70,000 soldiers of Robert E. Lee's

Gettysburg National Military Park, Gettysburg, Pennsylvania.

The 72nd Pennsylvania memorial, Gettysburg National Military Park, Pennsylvania.

Army of Northern Virginia faced 93,000 Federal troops of the Army of the Potomac, under its newly appointed commander, George Meade.

For the first day and a half, fortune shone on the Rebels. The Northern troops retreated through Gettysburg and were forced back along the center and left. In mid-afternoon of July 2, two Southern regiments occupied the Round Top, a wooded hill at the southern end of the Union line, and, joined by three other regiments, were ordered to occupy the undefended Little Round Top just to the north, thereby making Meade's entire position untenable.

But Brig. Gen. Gouverneur K. Warren, the army's chief engineer, had discovered that the crucial height was empty and alerted Meade. A Union brigade reached its summit with only 15 minutes to spare, just in time to turn back the advancing Confederates. Today Warren's statue crowns Little Round Top, where, proving that history is made not only by processes but also by individuals, he saved the Union.

The third day of the battle is known for Pickett's Charge, in which, after a heated artillery exchange, 12,000 Confederate troops attacked the Union center. A hundred or so broke through, but the charge was repulsed, having claimed more than 5,000 Southern casualties in the space of an hour. From that moment on it was ebb tide for the Southern cause.

In the North, Gettysburg evokes chiefly the address delivered by Lincoln four months later at the dedication of the cemetery there. For the South, it is epitomized by Pickett's Charge, which became part of the mythology of the Old South. Southern boys, novelist William Faulkner suggests, have dreamed of playing their part in the war and perhaps with their heroic deeds, changing history.

The two armies suffered more than 50,000 casualties at Gettysburg, including nearly 7,000 dead. It was bloodshed on a scale unprecedented on the North American continent, an epic of heroism and cowardice, foolhardy gestures and the fortunes of war. In the end, perhaps Rhett Butler was right: Pickett's Charge failed in part because the Southern batteries ran low on ammunition before the Union cannon did. On the other hand, were it not for Warren's vigilance, that would not have mattered.

THE GETTYSBURG ADDRESS

Fourscore and seven years ago our fathers brought forth on this continent a new nation, conceived in liberty and dedicated to the proposition that all men are created equal.

Now we are engaged in a great civil war, testing whether that nation, or any nation so conceived and so dedicated, can long endure. We are met on a great battlefield of that war. We have come to dedicate a portion of that field as a final resting-place for those who here gave their lives that that nation might live. It is altogether fitting and proper that we should do this. But, in a larger sense, we cannot dedicate—we cannot consecrate—we cannot hallow—this ground. The brave men, living and dead, who struggled here have consecrated it, far above our poor power to add or detract. The world will little note, nor long remember what we say here, but it can never forget what they did here. It is for us the living, rather, to be dedicated here to the unfinished work which they who fought here have thus far so nobly advanced. It is rather for us to be here dedicated to the great task remaining before us—that from these honored dead we take increased devotion to that cause for which they gave the last full measure of devotion—that we here highly resolve that these dead shall not have died in vain—that this nation, under God, shall have a new birth of freedom and that government of the people, by the people, for the people, shall not perish from the earth.

—President Abraham Lincoln, November 19, 1863

VICKSBURG

Union Victory & Command of the Mississippi River

"Vicksburg is the key. The War can never be brought to a close until the key is in our pocket."
—President Abraham Lincoln, November 1861

VICKSBURG, MISSISSIPPI

In the mid-19th century, the Mississippi River was the main trunk of the United States, linking the Midwest to the port of New Orleans and thence to Europe. Thomas Jefferson had observed that any country in possession of New Orleans was the natural enemy of the United States. Thus, political and moral arguments aside, commercial interests prevented the North from acquiescing in Southern independence.

The Union's grand strategy focused on blockading Southern ports and regaining control of the Mississippi. By June 1862 Union forces had moved southward from Kentucky and taken Memphis. Moving northward from the Gulf of Mexico, David Farragut's fleet had captured New Orleans, Baton Rouge, and Natchez. When Farragut's gunboats approached Vicksburg in May, its commander breathed defiance: "Mississippians don't know, and refuse to learn, how to surrender to an enemy." The town, on a bluff high above a hairpin bend in the river, which its heavy guns dominated, proved impregnable from the waterside. Farragut soon withdrew his vessels.

Lincoln referred to Vicksburg as the key: "The war can never be brought to a close until that key is in our pocket." Jefferson Davis concurred, calling it the "nail head that holds the South's two halves together."

Between November 1862 and March 1863, Maj. Gen. Ulysses Grant, the Union commander in the west, made seven attempts to advance troops to the landward side of Vicksburg; seven times he failed.

Blessed with patient superiors and almost unlimited human resources and materiel, Grant tried again. On March 29 he sent troops marching through the mud on the west side of the Mississippi to get them downstream of Vicksburg.

To cross the river, the troops would require the protection of gunboats. The commander of the Mississippi River flotilla, Rear Adm. David Porter, told Grant he could get his craft past Vicksburg but could not return them upstream should this eighth attempt fail. Grant did not hesitate. On the night of April 16, seven gunboats and three supply ships ran the gauntlet (one of the latter was sunk), followed by six more transports a week later.

The Confederate batteries foiled the first attempt to get the infantry across the river, at Grand Gulf on April 29. The next day, learning of a good road at Bruinsberg, Grant ordered a new attempt there. Some 17,000 troops landed unopposed on April 30–May 1.

Instead of striking north for Vicksburg, Grant moved northeast toward Jackson, which his soldiers entered on May 14. From there he turned west. His victory over the outnumbered Confederates at Champion Hill on May 16 and at Big Black River the next day opened the road to Vicksburg.

Hoping to capitalize on Confederate demoralization, Grant ordered frontal assaults on the heavily fortified town on May 19 and again on May 22. Both times

Massachusetts State Memorial, the first state memorial erected within Vicksburg National Military Park, Mississippi, cost $4,500 and was dedicated on November 14, 1903. The statue, sculpted by Theo Alice Ruggles Kitson, is mounted on a 15-ton boulder from Massachusetts.

Missouri State Memorial, Vicksburg National Military Park, Mississippi. This is the only state memorial on the battlefield dedicated to soldiers of both armies. Its height symbolizes 42 Missouri units: 27 Union and 15 Confederate. It stands where opposing Missouri regiments clashed in battle.

his men suffered bloody repulses. After that the Union forces, which outnumbered the garrison two to one, settled down for a prolonged siege. Day after day they bombarded the city, forcing many of its 4,500 citizens to take shelter in caves. Day after day the besiegers moved their trenches closer to the Confederate lines. Day after day the food supplies in the beleaguered town dwindled. Confederate Lieut. Gen. John C. Pemberton and his garrison of 30,000 held on tenaciously, hoping vainly that a relief force might appear in Grant's rear and compel him to raise the siege.

After 47 days in the trenches, Pemberton asked for terms. Grant began by demanding unconditional surrender. Then, recognizing the gallantry of his foe, he agreed to parole the officers and men until they could be exchanged. Vicksburg surrendered on July 4, 1863.

Five days later, the Confederate garrison at Port Hudson, 240 miles downriver, also raised the white flag. The Mississippi was in Union hands for its entire length. As Lincoln put it in August, "the Father of Waters again goes unvexed to the sea."

APPOMATTOX

Confederates Surrender to Union Army, Ending the Civil War

"General, this is deeply humiliating; but I console myself that the whole country will rejoice at this day's business."—a Confederate during the surrender ceremony, April 12, 1865

MCLEAN HOUSE, APPOMATTOX, VIRGINIA

When Ulysses S. Grant took over the Army of the Potomac, in March 1864, he enjoyed a freedom from political interference denied to his predecessors. And unlike Robert E. Lee, commanding the Confederate Army of Northern Virginia, he had almost unlimited reserves of manpower and materiel.

Grant kept pounding away at Lee's lines, absorbing heavy losses without flinching. After each bloody repulse his army sidled southward, forcing Lee to follow suit until he had been pushed back to Richmond.

By fall, three of the four railroads supplying the Confederate capital had been cut. All winter Grant extended his position, forcing Lee to thin his already fragile lines to keep from being outflanked.

The final assault on the Confederate right began on March 29. On April 1, at Five Forks, Union forces overran the Confederate positions and cut the Southside Railroad. Lee ordered the evacuation of Richmond and Petersburg on the night of April 2–3.

His plan was to steal a day's march on the Union troops and pick up supplies en route. But at Amelia Court House, discovering that the anticipated rations had not been shipped from Richmond, Lee allowed his hungry men a day to forage. By giving Grant time to catch up, this snafu sealed the Confederates' fate. The gray troops, still unfed, resumed their march that night, hoping to link up with Joseph Johnston's Army of Tennessee, retreating northward from North Carolina.

Union commander Ulysses S. Grant's desk at the McLean House, Appomattox, Virginia.

McLean house, Appomattox, Virginia. On April 9, 1865 the Confederate Army commander Robert E. Lee met Union Army commander Ulysses S. Grant in the parlor of the Wilmer McLean house at Appomattox, Virginia, and surrendered. The house became a sensation after the surrender. In 1893 it was dismantled for display in Washington, D.C. But that never happened, and the National Park Service reconstructed the building on its original site in the 1940s. The home is near the Appomattox Courthouse.

Supplies were waiting at Farmville on April 7, but the fast-marching bluecoats arrived before the famished Southerners could enjoy them. They resumed their retreat, unaware that a Union column was marching by a shorter route to block their path.

On April 8, the Confederates bivouacked a mile from Appomattox Station. That night, artillery fire and the glow of Union campfires told them they were surrounded. A gallant dawn attempt to break out was turned back.

At 11 A.M. Lee notified Grant that he was ready to surrender. A little after 1 P.M. Lee entered the home of the McLean family in the tiny hamlet of Appomattox. Grant arrived half an hour later. By 3 P.M. the terms of capitulation had been arranged.

Three days later, the Army of Northern Virginia formally laid down its arms, starting a domino effect. On April 26, Johnston surrendered near Durham, North Carolina. On May 4, Richard Taylor surrendered the 10,000 Confederates in Alabama and Mississippi. On June 2, Kirby Smith signed the capitulation of Confederate forces west of the Mississippi. Cherokee chief Stand Watie surrendered the last Confederate army in the field on June 23.

On May 10, President Andrew Johnson proclaimed that "armed resistance to the authority of this government…may be regarded as virtually at an end." This, the Supreme Court later held, marked the legal end of the war.

The CSS *Shenandoah*, unaware of developments ashore, continued to prey on Union shipping. On June 22, in the Bering Sea, it fired the last shot of the war, at a New Bedford whaler. When its captain, James Waddell, finally learned that the Confederacy was no more, he resolved to run for England. On November 6, the *Shenandoah* steamed proudly into Liverpool and an official Confederate flag was lowered for the last time.

In four years of hostilities, 365,000 Northern and 256,000 Southern soldiers had perished—in battle, of their wounds, of disease, or of noncombat causes. One of ten able-bodied northern men was dead or incapacitated, and one of four in the South.

As a consequence of the war, hundreds of thousands of men who had never been as far as the next county saw other states and encountered other Americans. For the first time they experienced their country and learned that they all spoke the same language, worshipped the same God, and espoused pretty much the same values. In the aftermath of the bloody conflict, these United States finally became the United States.

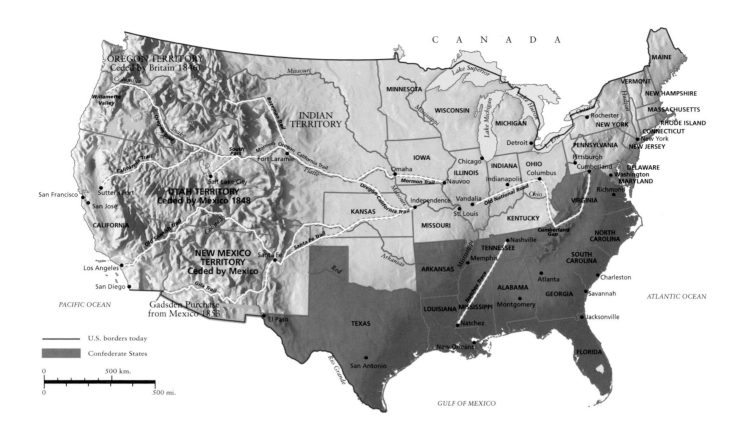

THE CONFEDERACY (1861–1865)

Confederate states on the map appear in orange.

In 1861, South Carolina was the first state to secede from the United States at the outset of the Civil War. The states of Mississippi, Florida, Alabama, Georgia, and Texas seceded about a month later; followed by Virginia, Arkansas, North Carolina, and Tennessee in the months following. After the conflict ended, with Confederate commander Robert E. Lee's surrender to Union commander Ulysses S. Grant in 1865 in Appomattox, states that fought under the Confederate flag were readmitted to the United States from 1866 to 1870. The first to rejoin was Tennessee, and the last, Georgia. Some states delayed freeing resident slaves after the Emancipation Proclamation.

CONFEDERATE STATES IN THE CIVIL WAR

Capital, Richmond, Virginia
Jefferson Davis, President

SECESSION OF AMERICAN STATES

State	Secession Date	Readmission Date
South Carolina	December 20, 1860	June 25, 1868
Mississippi	January 9, 1851	February 23, 1870
Florida	January 10, 1861	June 25, 1868
Alabama	January 11, 1861	June 25, 1868
Georgia	January 19, 1861	June 25, 1868
second readmission		July 15, 1870
Louisiana	January 25, 1861	June 25, 1868
Texas	February 1, 1861	March 30, 1870
Virginia	April 17, 1861	February 23, 1870
Arkansas	May 6, 1861	June 22, 1868
North Carolina	May 20, 1861	June 25, 1868
Tennessee	June 8, 1861	July 24, 1866

GOLDEN SPIKE
Union Pacific & Central Pacific Railroads' East-West Meet

"Railroad iron is a magician's rod, in its power to evoke the sleeping energies of land and water."
—Ralph Waldo Emerson, February 7, 1844

BRIGHAM CITY AND PROMONTORY, UTAH, AND COUNCIL BLUFFS, IOWA

The extension of U.S. territory to the Pacific in 1848 spurred politicians and capitalists to dream of a transcontinental railroad. At least nine possible routes were surveyed; Southerners naturally preferred a southern route; Northerners, a northern one. Secession left the latter a free hand. The Pacific Railroad Act of 1862 specified a northern route through the Platte River Valley and stipulated that two companies would build it—the Central Pacific eastward from Sacramento and the Union Pacific westward from Iowa. Congress authorized the president to select the actual terminus. Lincoln, perhaps remembering his visit to Council Bluffs in 1859, when he discussed the transcontinental railroad project with Grenville Dodge, chose that town in 1863. The Union Pacific established its headquarters across the Missouri River in Omaha.

The only town in the 1,700 miles from there to Sacramento was at Salt Lake. The railroad would join what were essentially two separate countries across the empty (except for Indians and bison) plains, mountains, and deserts. Most industrial inputs for the Central Pacific—locomotives, rails, cars, and wheels—had to be shipped out around Cape Horn, a voyage that took five to six months.

In the 19th century, with the growth of the transcontinental railroad and tracks linking many cities and towns, many steam-engine trains like this one criss-crossed the continent. Courtesy of Greenfield Village, Dearborn, Michigan.

Construction was financed by grants of land along the right-of-way to the two companies, which resold plots to settlers and developers. When this proved inadequate, private investors were recruited.

Ground was broken at Omaha and Sacramento in 1863, but the first rails were not laid in Omaha until 1865. The Union Pacific hired Lincoln's old acquaintance Grenville Dodge, a logistics and engineering wizard for the Union army during the Civil War, as its chief engineer; he worked a similar miracle for the railroad. His major obstacle was not topography, however, but the hostility of the American Indian tribes, whose bison-dependent economy could not survive the iron horse and the flood of new settlers it would bring. Steady military pressure on the tribes and wanton extermination of the bison solved the problem.

Dodge pushed his men mercilessly. Paid an average of $1 a day, they worked 12 to 16 hours a day, seven days a week, laying one to three miles of track each day. Civil War veterans, Irish immigrants, and Appalachian mountaineers built the Union Pacific. The Central Pacific, with a much smaller population base and the harsh desert climate to contend with, found that Chinese coolies made the best workers (ultimately they composed 90% of the workforce).

The Central Pacific, which had to cross the Sierra Nevada and endure more severe winters, ended up building 742 miles to the Union Pacific's 1,038. They met at Promontory Point, Utah, on May 10, 1869. The ceremony, attended by senior representatives of the two lines, who pounded silver and gold spikes into the last rails, was "broadcast live" over the telegraph by Western Union. Construction had taken three years, six months, and ten days. Soon it would take only ten days to travel from San Francisco to New York.

Fourteen years later, when a parallel line, the Northern Pacific, met itself west of Helena, in Montana Territory, it staged an even more impressive ceremony, featuring former president Ulysses Grant. A Crow chief, Iron Bull, delivered the last speech, in sign language, sadly admitting that when he drove the golden spike home he would also be sounding the death knell of the Indian sway over North America.

Golden Spike Monument, Council Bluffs, Iowa. This 56-foot concrete replica of the golden spike marks the eastern terminus of the Union Pacific railroad. This overgrown imitation of the actual golden spike of 1869 was erected in 1939 to mark the world premiere (in Omaha, not Council Bluffs) of Cecil B. DeMille's film Union Pacific, *a fictional account of the building of the transcontinental railroad.*

WEST VIRGINIA COAL MINES

Miners in a Company Town

APPALACHIA—WEST VIRGINIA, WESTERN PENNSYLVANIA, AND EASTERN KENTUCKY

Coal mining in North America began in the second half of the 18th century in western Pennsylvania, where the outcroppings and near-surface deposits could be dug easily. This was the tip of the largest coalfield in the world, stretching beneath the Ohio River basin, with its richest veins in Appalachia—West Virginia and eastern Kentucky. Initially coal was mined only for local use or special applications that required a higher-energy fuel than wood.

Starting in the 1840s, and especially after the Civil War, coal fueled the railroads, which in turn made it possible to transport coal cheaply to serve as a primary energy source all over the country. Factories, no longer dependent on waterpower, could be sited to take advantage of the availability of raw materials and labor. By the end of the century, coal-burning power plants had ushered in the electrical era.

Early mining operations were small local initiatives, but much of the industry was soon swallowed up by outside corporations—railways, steelmakers, utilities—that bought up mineral rights cheaply and dug Appalachian coal for their own use. Within two or three generations, the families that had once tilled the surface of the land were working underneath it for wages.

Beckley exhibition mine, Raleigh County, West Virginia. Beckley, in operation from 1891 to 1991, and other mines throughout Raleigh County have produced 792 million tons of bituminous coal. County mines employed as many as 14,226 people annually.

Because most mines were inaccessible from existing hamlets, the companies built their own towns, with rental housing for miners, a company store, a hospital, and other amenities. Miners were often paid in scrip that could be spent only at the company store, whose prices reflected its monopolistic position. Most miners were in perpetual debt to the company and thus unable to quit and find other jobs. With no alternative employment available locally, their sons either migrated to northern cities or followed their fathers into the mines, perpetuating the cycle of poverty, peril, and disease. This arrangement was the closest to feudalism that the United States has ever known. Appalachia was the poorest region in the country.

Miners fought a long and bitter battle to unionize. The establishment—government, churches, press—sided with the owners. Strikers were evicted from company-owned housing, denied use of company-run health

Mining village with company houses, Elkhorn, McDowell County, West Virginia.

facilities, barred from the company store. The local police—also company employees—kept labor organizers away and intimidated miners who tried to join the union. Union members were dealt with harshly if they attacked strikebreakers or company property; company goons generally clubbed and shot with impunity. Coal wars, pitting desperate strikers against owners and scabs, were common.

The United Mine Workers had some success early in the 20th century, but it took New Deal legislation of the 1930s to protect workers' rights adequately. Only after World War II did the companies relax their grip and allow the camps to become towns whose residents enjoyed democratic rights.

Deep mining is a dirty and dangerous job. Miners frequently spend their entire shift stooped over a narrow seam of coal or kneeling in a puddle of water. They are prey to floods, fires, poison gases, cave-ins, and explosions. Until recently, if they survived these calamities they could look forward to the slow, suffocating agony of "black lung," the progressive destruction of the air sacs in the lungs by inhaled coal dust.

Mining wreaks havoc on the environment, too. Acid drainage from deep mines is still a major source of water pollution. Surface mining blights the countryside with ugly scars.

Repairing this ravaged human and natural landscape was part of Lyndon Johnson's Great Society program in the mid-1960s. Government antipoverty funds flowed to Appalachia. Tough federal and state legislation required coal companies to invest in reclamation and compensate workers for black lung–related disability and death. This stimulated the development and use of advanced technology to protect workers and reduce pollution. As a result, by the end of the 20th century coal mining was much safer and environmentally friendlier, and Appalachia was no longer a shameful pocket of poverty in the center of the richest country on earth.

SAN FRANCISCO
Paper Sons at the Golden Gate

GOLDEN GATE BRIDGE, ANGEL ISLAND, SAN FRANCISCO, CALIFORNIA

Few small bodies of water encompass so many dreams and so many tears as San Francisco Bay and the inlet leading to it. The Spanish, who discovered the bay in 1769, established a *presidio* or fortress garrison on its southern shore in 1776. But they never gave the three-mile channel between the ocean and the bay a name of its own. That had to wait for John C. Frémont, at the time a lieutenant in the U.S. Army. When he first sailed into the inlet in 1846 he called it *Chrysopylae*—Greek for "golden gate"—because it reminded him of the entrance to the "back bay" of Constantinople, the Golden Horn. Since fewer and fewer Americans were being educated in classical Greek, it was the English version of the name that stuck.

The Golden Gate soon became the western entrance to the land of opportunity. Among those arriving through it were Chinese immigrants attracted by the glittering discovery at Sutter's Mill. Thousands followed to what they called *Gam Saan* or "Gold Mountain." Although they were not officially enslaved, laws and socioeconomic pressures channeled them into the dirtiest and worst-paying jobs—notably the construction of the transcontinental railway.

Golden Gate Bridge, San Francisco, California.

One consequence of the depression of the 1870s—the worst the United States had yet known—was the Chinese Exclusion Act of 1882, which suspended the admission of Chinese laborers and barred further nationalization of Chinese. Only persons whose fathers or husbands were already U.S. citizens were allowed entry. This gave rise to "paper sons," who often paid large sums to acquire false documentation of a filial relationship to a U.S. citizen. The San Francisco earthquake and fire of 1906, which destroyed many original birth and citizenship records, facilitated the scam. Trying to enforce the law, the Immigration Bureau interrogated almost all Chinese who arrived at the country's ports, as well as their putative parents, witnesses, and others.

The interrogation process was a game of cat-and-mouse in which the interrogators tried to catch the would-be immigrants in an inconsistency, while the immigrants, who had frequently spent their voyage across the Pacific conning "coaching papers" about their ostensible parents, home villages, etc., tried to outlast them.

Pershing Square, Presidio of San Francisco, California.

In 1910, a new processing station was opened on Angel Island in San Francisco Bay. Although billed as the Ellis Island of the West, the Immigration Service referred to it privately as the "Guardian of the Western Gate," since its main function was to enforce the Exclusion Act. During the next 30 years, more than a million immigrants—Asians, South and Central Americans, Europeans, and Australians—were processed by Angel Island personnel. Most were admitted without delay and only their papers spent more than a few hours on the island.

But for 175,000 Chinese immigrants (and more than 100,000 Japanese), Angel Island was a detention camp where they spent an average of two to three weeks. About 20 to 25% were denied entry and sent back home. The Angel Island Station was closed after a fire in 1940. The Exclusion Act was repealed in 1943.

Another island in the bay is Alcatraz. Fortified in the 1850s as part of the harbor defenses, it also served as a military stockade. Later it was transferred to civilian control for use as a maximum-security prison. The prison was in operation for only 29 years (1934–1963), but the "Rock" assumed mythical proportions.

The Presidio became the most important U.S. military installation on the West Coast. It played a support role in every American war between 1848 and 1994, when it was decommissioned. Compensating for the tears of those imprisoned and detained is the Golden Gate Bridge, completed in 1937. With its soaring arches and gleaming towers, the bridge is an inspiring emblem of humanity's ability to overcome natural obstacles and create beauty at the same time.

Since the mid-19th century, San Francisco has been America's major port for conducting trade with Asia.

YELLOWSTONE

Wildlife Refuges, Nature Preserves & the National Parks Movement

YELLOWSTONE NATIONAL PARK IN IDAHO, MONTANA, AND WYOMING

The town green or commons was a feature of European towns and villages and had been included in New England town planning from the beginning. Philadelphia was also laid out with green preserves. But the town green began as a place for cows to graze and the commons was exceptional for colonial towns. Greenery was taken for granted; it was civilization that needed planning. Only in the generation before the Civil War did city dwellers begin to feel a need to set aside undeveloped land for urban parks.

An early urban romantic park was Manhattan's Central Park, authorized in 1853. Frederick Law Olmsted, its superintendent and designer, left New York ten years later for the California estate of Gen. John C. Frémont, where he was exposed to the remarkable landscape of the Yosemite Valley and the Big Trees. Capitalizing on a groundswell of interest in preserving these wonders, Olmsted encouraged influential Californians to lobby Congress. In 1864 it ceded the "Yo-Semite Valley" and "Mariposa Big Tree Grove" to the State of California, which was to reserve them in perpetuity "for public use, resort, and recreation."

The first European to see the Yellowstone region was probably John Colter, in 1808. The earliest written account of its natural wonders appeared in a Philadelphia newspaper in 1827 but was dismissed as the wild

American buffalo (bison), Madison River, Yellowstone National Park.

ravings of an overheated imagination. Eventually, however, its geysers and hot springs, the Grand Canyon of the Yellowstone River, fossil forests, waterfalls, and wealth of fauna attracted curious visitors.

A number of survey and prospecting expeditions explored the Yellowstone in 1869–1872 (the prospectors, fortunately, found little gold) and spread reports of its wonders. The last of these was commissioned by Congress. Its 500-page report persuaded the lawmakers that the region had little economic potential and spurred them in 1872 to establish Yellowstone National Park—2.2 million acres of wilderness "reserved and withdrawn from settlement, occupancy, or sale...and set apart...for the benefit and enjoyment of the people" and "for the preservation, from injury or spoliation, of all timber, mineral deposits, natural curiosities, or wonders...and their retention in their natural condition."

But Yosemite and Yellowstone were exceptional. Americans felt their country was blessed with so much land and so many resources that they could never be exhausted. According to Gifford Pinchot, in 1890 "the nation was obsessed by a fury of development. The American Colossus was fiercely intent on appropriating and exploiting the riches of the richest of all continents."

Geyser, Yellowstone National Park.

Conservation, the idea of husbanding resources in a way that best serves every aspect of human well-being for the nation at large, rather than enriching a few property owners and developers, was planted in the American reality by two stubborn men. Pinchot, the first professionally trained forester in the United States, became head of the Division of Forestry in the Agriculture Department in 1898. Three years later his approach received strong backing at the very top when Theodore Roosevelt—who knew and loved the West from his brief stint as a Dakota rancher—became president.

These two men abhorred the no-thought-for-tomorrow despoliation of nature in the pursuit of private profit. Yellowstone had been reserved as a national park only because it seemed to have no other use. Pinchot and Roosevelt were the first to insist that natural beauty and recreation have intrinsic value that can outweigh the monetary value of exploiting resources. As president, Roosevelt established the U.S. Forest Service, proclaimed eighteen national monuments, and authorized the founding of five national parks, 51 wildlife refuges, and 150 national forests.

In 1916, President Woodrow Wilson signed legislation establishing the National Park Service as part of the Department of the Interior, to "conserve the scenery and the natural and historic objects and the wild life therein and to provide for the enjoyment for the same in such manner and by such means as will leave them unimpaired for the enjoyment of future generations."

In 1892 Adirondacks Park was declared "forever wild" by the New York state legislature. At 9,375 square miles, the Adirondacks is the largest park, federal or state, in the United States outside Alaska.

In colonial times, the Iroquois and Algonquins claimed the region. Later Ethan Allen and the Green Mountain boys took Fort Ticonderoga on Lake George from the English in 1775. The first American navy fought the British army invasion from Canada on Lake Champlain in 1776.

DODGE CITY
Law & Order in the West

"Fast is fine, but accuracy is everything."—Wyatt Earp

DODGE CITY, KANSAS, NEAR THE SANTA FE TRAIL

Dodge City was not really founded by the movies and fostered by television—even though, relative to population, it has been the setting for more movies and series than any other place in the United States. In fact, during its brief heyday, the real Dodge City was far more open—but less bloody—than anything that television could allow Matt Dillon to be involved in.

For six decades after 1821, the Santa Fe Trail, running from Missouri to New Mexico, was one of the most important routes for westward migration and two-way commerce. To protect the wagon trains from the ravages of the Kiowa, Cheyenne, and other Native American tribes, who were fighting a rearguard battle to protect their hunting grounds against the invaders from the east, in 1865 the U.S. Army established Fort Dodge in southwestern Kansas, about 150 miles west of Wichita, near where the Santa Fe Trail split into the northern Mountain Branch and the shorter but arid Cimarron Cutoff.

In 1871, Henry Sitler built himself a sod house at his cattle ranch five miles west of the fort. Before the next year was out, Sitler had more neighbors than he had ever imagined in his worst nightmares, including two general stores, three dance halls, and six saloons—not to mention the Atchison, Topeka & Santa Fe railroad, which made the town's fortune.

Over the next three years, while hunters slaughtered the vast herds of plains bison, Dodge City was the bison capital of the West, shipping out some 850,000 hides. By 1875, however, the bison were almost gone, along with the native tribes that had depended on them for food. The town's economy switched to another bovine

Statue at the entrance to Dodge City, Kansas.

species, longhorn cattle, which were brought on the hoof from their Texas rangelands to the railhead in huge cattle drives.

Millions of head of cattle passed through Dodge City over the next 15 years, en route to Chicago, Kansas City, and other meatpacking centers. Drovers charged $1 to $1.50 a head to walk animals north from Texas. Even the arrival of the railroad in northern Texas (1873) did not undercut their business at first, because freight rates were several times higher.

The drives made ten to fifteen miles a day, bringing the grazing cattle to market in about six weeks. Bad weather, stampedes, and flooded rivers posed the major dangers. In the real world, as opposed to the movies, most drovers did not carry guns on the trail, because they were liable to go off accidentally and frighten the cattle.

Dodge City became a boomtown, the main R&R center for men who led a danger-

Boot Hill Museum and Front Street, Dodge City, Kansas. This western history village museum, a reconstruction of Dodge City in 1876, is located on the original site of Boot Hill Cemetery in downtown Dodge City.

ous and lonely life, many of them frustrated veterans of the Confederate army. They were hard drinkers and high-stakes gamblers, quick to take insult, almost as quick to fire their sidearms. In 1876, when the town had a permanent population of 1,200, nineteen establishments had liquor licenses. Gambling dens and bordellos were unlicensed and uncountable.

Law enforcement was an almost hopeless task. The respectable citizens solved the problem of guaranteeing their personal safety by dividing the town into two zones. North of the railroad there was a strictly enforced ban on wearing or carrying firearms; south of it, the forces of law and order lay low and let nature take its course.

In 1885, Kansas and other northern states imposed a total quarantine on out-of-state livestock to prevent the spread of Texas fever. This, plus the introduction of winter wheat and resultant enclosure of the land, put an end to the cattle drives. But this brief interlude and relatively small stretch of the southern plains were transmuted into the Wild West of American folk history: cowboys and Indians, drovers and farmers, gunmen and lawmen, gamblers and prostitutes, posses and vigilantes, the marshal or sheriff standing alone on the deserted main street, and the U.S. cavalry riding to the rescue.

SANTA FE TRAIL

William Becknell, a trader from Franklin, Missouri, blazed the Santa Fe Trail by following the well-known route along the Missouri River via the Kansas and Arkansas Rivers. When he reached La Juna, Colorado, he had had little success in trapping and trading. He then turned southwest on an old Indian trail along Timpas Creek, across the Ratan Pass, down to the Canadian River, and arrived at Santa Fe, New Mexico. Since Mexico had recently won its independence from Spain, most Spanish traders had left the territory, and Mexicans were anxious to trade with Becknell and other Americans.

The Santa Fe Trail was used from 1821 to about 1880. During the Mexican War, it served as a military road leading to the Southwest, and during the gold rush, prospectors and pioneers followed the route to California. Beginning near Kansas City, Missouri, the trail led west to Fort Dodge, Kansas, where it forked, one route going west and one going southwest to Santa Fe, New Mexico.

LITTLE BIGHORN
Crazy Horse Meets Custer

"On the 5th of July—for it took that time for the news to come—the sun rose on a beautiful world, but with its earliest beams came the first knell of disaster. A steamer came down the river bearing the wounded from the battle of the Little Big Horn, of Sunday, June 25th. This battle wrecked the lives of twenty-six women at Fort Lincoln, and orphaned children of officers and soldiers joined their cry to that of their bereaved mothers."
—from Elizabeth B. Custer's memoir *Boots & Saddles* (1885); Elizabeth was Col. Custer's wife

CROW INDIAN RESERVATION, MONTANA

The aboriginal inhabitants of North America, whom Europeans called Indians, comprised some 200 separate tribes who warred incessantly among themselves. Almost all of them had a tribal and heroic culture that was the antithesis of the individualism and pragmatism of their rivals for possession of the continent.

The eastern nations had no chance against European firearms and germs, which devastated or wiped out entire tribes. The whites pressed the natives back, purchase after land grab, massacre after battle, and treaty after broken treaty, until, by the end of the 1830s, almost none remained east of the Mississippi.

But here the westward expansion stalled because of the opposition of the tribes of the Great Plains and Southwest, who could shoot twenty arrows from their galloping horses while a soldier loaded his rifle and got off a single round.

The process began anew after the Civil War. The transcontinental railroad was being built to link California and Oregon to the rest of the country. With slavery no longer an issue, the country could turn its attention to the

Last Stand Hill, Little Bighorn battlefield, Montana. On this knoll, Custer and about 41 men shot their horses for breastworks and stood against the American Indians, who were also defending their right to live in lands America claimed.

Custer National Cemetery. Little Bighorn Battlefield National Monument, Montana.

open frontier and the problem of the other non-European people on the continent. And one of the technological advances of the war had been the repeating carbine, which restored the firepower advantage of the U.S. cavalry.

The army tended to believe that stern force would keep the tribes in line. Easterners, at their safe distance, generally favored a policy of peaceful accommodation. Both saw sedentarizing and Christianizing the natives— in essence, turning them into white men—as the solution. The settlers on the frontier, who suffered the depredations of a cruel foe that expected and offered no quarter, took a different line: extermination.

Under the Grant administration (1869–1877), which alternated between force and accommodation, well-intentioned Federal commissioners were sent to negotiate with important tribes. Major chiefs were brought east to press their case and familiarize the general public with their needs. Ultimately, however, no accommodation was possible, because the American Indians could never accept the presence of railroads, which disrupted the bison herds on which they depended. And the railroad was the essential infrastructure for American prosperity.

There were massacres by Indians of travelers and settlers who had invaded their ancestral lands, and massacres by settlers and soldiers of peaceful Indian encampments. Public opinion (except on the frontier) was frequently outraged by the latter. The greatest leaders of the Native American resistance have found a place in the American pantheon, including the Apache Cochise, Chief Joseph of the Nez Percé, and even Crazy Horse, the Oglala chieftain who wiped out a detachment of the 7th Cavalry, commanded by the flamboyant Col. George Armstrong Custer, at Little Big Horn (in Montana Territory) on June 25, 1876.

Custer did everything wrong: he rode out in search of glory rather than to accomplish his assigned military goals, ignored explicit orders, and divided his forces without knowing the enemy's strength. In fact, he was facing what may have been the largest encampment of Plains Indians ever—more than 3,000 warriors—against a force that numbered about 650 before he split it into three parts. Two of the units eventually found each other and held out against their attackers, suffering fifty dead and fifty wounded. Custer's 200 officers, soldiers, scouts, and civilians were wiped out to the last man. News of the rout—the worst defeat ever suffered by the U.S. Army—reached Washington two days after the nation celebrated its centennial, putting a damper on the celebratory mood.

But Custer's "Last Stand" was also the last stand of the Plains Indians. Before the decade was over, all their tribes had been subdued and confined to reservations, soon to be followed by those of the Southwest.

STATUE OF LIBERTY
"Liberty Enlightening the World"

NEW YORK HARBOR, NEW YORK AND NEW JERSEY

Its official name is "Liberty Enlightening the World"—hence the torch raised high. Today the whole world knows it simply as the Statue of Liberty. The difference between the two is profound.

France—the Second Empire of Louis Napoleon, the supporter of Italian unification but also the prop of Pius IX in Rome and sponsor of Maximilian in Mexico—was itself in need of such enlightenment in 1865. That summer, a group of French liberals, moved by the Civil War that had just concluded with the emancipation of the slaves and the assassination of the Great Emancipator, floated the idea that France present the United States with a monument commemorating the bond between the two countries. Some years later, with the emperor in exile, Maximilian executed, and the Pope confined to the Vatican, one of the group's members, sculptor Frédéric Auguste Bartholdi, sailed for New York to study the feasibility of the project. The idea for the colossus was born, he later recalled, as his ship entered New York Harbor.

Statue of Liberty, New York Harbor, New York. The figure of a woman with a lamp enlightening the world was a well known symbol in earlier centuries.

Bartholdi's design is full of symbolism: Liberty tramples on the broken shackles of tyranny—denoting freedom from nonrepresentative government. The tablet in her left hand is inscribed with the date "July 4, 1776," alluding to the Declaration of Independence with its rejection of monarchy and proclamation of the inalienable rights of "life, liberty, and the pursuit of happiness." The torch held high, toward the east, offers enlightenment—knowledge that is simultaneously the prerequisite for and the greatest benefit of freedom—to the countries of the Old World. This is how both the donor and recipient understood the statue in the late 19th century.

Statue of Liberty and Manhattan skyline, New York, New York. The Statue of Liberty has become a symbol for all that is American. Perhaps no other monument, place, or physical object, except the flag, evokes as much pride and sense of national identity.

The "renaming" of the monument and new interpretation of its meaning can be traced to Emma Lazarus's now-famous sonnet, "The New Colossus." Lazarus (1849–1887) wrote it in 1883 for the portfolio of the Art Loan Collection that was sold to raise funds for the construction of the pedestal on which the statue was erected. At the time it did not attract particular attention. Lazarus was not invited to the dedication of the statue on October 15, 1886 (nor were any women, except for Bartholdi's wife and the young daughter of Ferdinand de Lesseps of the French committee, who was one of the keynote speakers). When a bronze plaque bearing the poem was mounted in the Statue in 1903, it was the contribution of a private donor. It was only in later years, when the perceived meaning of the statue changed, that the poem assumed the emblematic status it has today.

Lazarus's reference to the statue as the "Mother of Exiles," extending "world-wide welcome" and challenging the Old World to keep its "storied pomp" while giving America its "huddled masses yearning to breathe free," turned the torch from a source of illumination for distant shores, inspiring their people to institute freedom there, into a beacon guiding those en route to join the already-free people of America: "I lift my lamp beside the golden door."

Thus "Liberty Enlightening the World," a monument to the political thinkers of 1776 and their practical achievement in designing a new form of government, became the Statue of Liberty, standing tall in New York Harbor, the gateway to the United States, overlooking the immigrants' first landfall on Ellis Island, a symbol of America as the magnet for the poor and oppressed.

"Not like the brazen giant of Greek fame,
With conquering limbs astride from land to land;
Here at our sea-washed, sunset gates shall stand
A mighty woman with a torch, whose flame
Is the imprisoned lightning, and her name
Mother of Exiles. From her beacon-hand
Glows world-wide welcome; her mild eyes command
The air-bridged harbor that twin cities frame.
'Keep, ancient lands, your storied pomp!' cries she
With silent lips. 'Give me your tired, your poor,
Your huddled masses yearning to breathe free,
The wretched refuse of your teeming shore,
Send these, the homeless, tempest-tossed to me,
I lift my lamp beside the golden door!'"
—Emma Lazarus, poem "The New Colossus" (1883)

ELLIS ISLAND
Immigrants at America's Eastern Gate

"Here is not merely a nation, but a teeming nation of nations."—Walt Whitman

CASTLE GARDEN IN NEW YORK HARBOR; NEW YORK AND NEW JERSEY

Although Congress passed the first Naturalization Act, which provided that "any alien, being a free white person, may be admitted to become a citizen of the United States," in 1790, immigration did not begin in earnest until several decades later. Push factors, like the economic dislocation caused by population growth, changes in land-use patterns, industrialization, the Irish potato famine, and the failed European revolutions of 1848, along with pull factors, like the discovery of gold in California, brought hundreds of thousands of immigrants to American shores before the Civil War. Their language or religion kept them from assimilating quickly. This set off the first wave of anti-immigrant agitation and the only one that coalesced into a major political move-

Ellis Island Immigration Museum, New York Harbor, New York and New Jersey.

ment—the American Party, better known as the Know Nothings, which reached its zenith in the 1850s. The Civil War, in which immigrants fought prominently on both sides, quelled this sentiment, to the point that the Republican platform of 1864 stated that "foreign immigration, which in the past has added so much to the wealth, resources, and increase of power to the nation...should be fostered and encouraged."

Before 1855, there was little or no inspection of immigrants. Newcomers simply passed through customs and entered the country. In August 1855, New York State opened the first immigrant-processing center at Castle Garden, an island off the southwest tip of Manhattan. Until its closure in 1890, more than 8 million people entered the United States there.

The rapid expansion after the Civil War, plus the shortening of the Atlantic crossing when steam power replaced sail, generated an immigration explosion from the mid-1870s on. During the 1880s, around 9% of the popu-

Looking for relatives on The American Immigrant Wall of Honor, which contains over 600,000 names of individuals and families who immigrated to the United States.

lation of Norway emigrated to America. The pogroms in Russia in 1881 sparked a wave of Jewish immigration.

Immigration came under Federal auspices in 1882. To cope with the flood of arrivals, the Federal government created the Bureau of Immigration in 1890 and constructed a new and larger reception station in New York. Ellis Island was opened on January 1, 1892.

Although there were other ports of entry, Ellis Island was the gateway to the Promised Land for the bulk of immigrant arrivals from 1892 until after World War I. Of the 27 million immigrants who entered the United States between 1880 and 1930, 20 million came through Ellis Island.

Ellis Island (and parallel facilities elsewhere) served to screen out "undesirables": the ill and infirm and persons of questionable social, economic, or moral fitness. Those who failed to pass the initial screening (up to 20% of the total) were detained on Ellis Island until an Immigration Board could review their cases. The Board was actually quite lenient; only 2% to 3% of all arrivals were ultimately denied entry and returned to their port of embarkation.

Ellis Island served as a center for processing immigrants to America from 1892 to 1943.

After World War I, anti-immigrant feeling rose again, some of it racially motivated, some inspired by the fear of Reds and anarchists that was triggered by a series of violent strikes and bombings. In 1921, the first Quota Act put an end to the open-door policy by limiting the annual admission of each national group to 3% of its representation in the 1910 census. The 1924 National Origins Act was even more draconian and limited immigration from any country to 2% of its representation in the 1890 census. The Act also encouraged prospective immigrants to undergo inspection at U.S. consulates in their countries of origin, making a stop on Ellis Island unnecessary. After July 1924, only those detained for hearings passed through Ellis Island.

Today, more than 100 million Americans can trace their antecedents to an immigrant who passed through the great Registry Room on Ellis Island.

KILL DEVIL HILLS, KITTY HAWK

America Takes Flight

"We were lucky enough to grow up in an environment where there was always much encouragement to children to pursue intellectual interests; to investigate whatever that aroused curiosity."
—Orville and Wilbur Wright

KILL DEVIL HILLS, KITTY HAWK, NORTH CAROLINA, AND DAYTON, OHIO

They were bicycle mechanics in an era when the bicycle was still a wonder of applied technology. But the Wright brothers of Dayton, Ohio, were bored by pedals; they dreamed of wings.

Neither Wilbur (born in 1867) nor Orville (four years younger) had more than a high-school education (Wilbur's plans to attend Yale were frustrated by injury and illness). That was not a major impediment, since most of the theory required had already been worked out and they merely needed to refine its implementation.

The wind-swept dunes of Kill Devil Hills, North Carolina, were the site of the Wright brothers' perfection of their first successful piloted aircraft. "The sunsets here are the prettiest I have ever seen. The clouds light up with all colors, in the background, with deep blue clouds of various shapes fringed with gold before."—Orville Wright

It may even have been an asset, because it enabled them to examine problems from a different perspective.

In 1896, Samuel Langley proved that a heavier-than-air craft could fly when two of his 30-pound steam-powered "aerodromes" stayed aloft for 75 and 90 seconds, covering 3,300 and 4,200 feet, respectively. Two essential components were lacking, though: a pilot and a steering system. The War Department and the Smithsonian Institute (Langley was its secretary) contributed $50,000 each to fund the next stage of his research.

Around that time Wilbur became intrigued by the idea of flight and infected his brother with the bug. They began collecting all the information available on the subject and spent the next four years mastering the existing body of theory and practice. Realizing that no one, including Langley, really knew how to make the final leap, the brothers decided to try their own hands at it.

By 1899 they were ready to attack the problem of controlling a craft in flight. Langley's designs relied on inherent stability. The Wrights, perhaps thinking about bicycles, concluded that dynamic stability, based on feedback between craft and pilot, was more promising. Wilbur came up with the idea of twisting the wings to rotate them and make the craft turn. They proved the idea—which eventually matured into ailerons—on a 5-foot kite.

Wright Brothers National Memorial, Kill Devil Hills, North Carolina. Kitty Hawk is nearby.

In 1900, they closed their shop and went to Kill Devil Hills, a chain of wind-swept dunes on one of the barrier islands between Albemarle Sound and the Atlantic Ocean in northern North Carolina. Their glider, with a wingspan of 17 feet, failed to generate the expected lift. The next year they continued their field trials with a 22-foot glider and discovered that the standard formulas for lift were wrong.

Back home in Dayton, they designed and built a wind tunnel in which they tested more than 50 airfoil sections to produce accurate lift tables. They used them to design a 32-foot glider, which they flew nearly a thousand times in North Carolina in the fall of 1902, and experimented with a movable tail linked to the ailerons until they were satisfied they could control the craft.

The last step was propulsion. The brothers commissioned a lightweight gasoline engine from mechanic Charles Taylor and used their wind tunnel to design a working propeller (their one real scientific achievement: they were the first to realize that a propeller is just a wing turned on its side).

Meanwhile, Langley's work was nearing completion. But his catapult-launched craft crashed in its two trials over the Potomac River, on October 7 and December 9, 1903.

Back in North Carolina, the Wright brothers tested their 40-foot, 600-pound Flyer I, the culmination of a project in which they had invested all of $1,000. Wilbur piloted the first attempt, on December 14, but oversteered the craft into the ground. Three days later it was Orville's turn. At 10:35 A.M. he began the historic flight, covering 120 feet in 12 seconds. A preset camera captured the moment for posterity. By day's end, in their fourth flight, Wilbur managed to fly 852 feet, keeping the craft aloft for 59 seconds, before a gust of wind crashed the craft beyond repair. There would be no more attempts that year. The brothers sent their father a telegram announcing their success from nearby Kitty Hawk—which thus became irrevocably linked to their achievement.

SUPREME COURT

"Equal Justice Under Law"

Today it is common to speak of the three co-equal branches of the American government—legislative, executive, and judicial. But that may not have been the Founders' intention.

Whereas Article One of the Constitution deals at length with Congress, its mode of election, and powers, and Article Two similarly defines the status of the President, Article Three states merely that "the judicial power of the United States shall be vested in one Supreme Court" and defines the scope of its jurisdiction.

It is Congress that decides when and where the Supreme Court sits and how many justices it has. The number of justices has fluctuated between five and ten; for most of its history the Court was a subtenant in the Capitol.

The immense authority of the Supreme Court, embodied in its power to declare Federal and state legislation unconstitutional, originates in the *Marbury v. Madison* decision of 1803. Ironically, here the Court ruled that a section of a 1789 law was null and void because Congress could not empower it to sit as a court of first

Supreme Court of the United States, Washington, D.C. "The Republic endures and this is the symbol of its faith," said Chief Justice Charles Evans Hughes at a ceremonial laying of the Supreme Court Building's cornerstone on October 13, 1932.

instance in cases other than those specified in the Constitution. This bold assertion of the principle of judicial review—which some but not all drafters of the Constitution thought implicit in it—was the work of Chief Justice John Marshall. During his 34 years on the bench, until his death in 1835, the Court enunciated the basic principles of the relations between the Federal government and the states. Under Congressional attack when Marshall first donned his judicial robes, by his death the Supreme Court had become a national institution that commanded respect and obedience.

This does not mean, of course, that every Supreme Court ruling has been greeted with understanding and respect. After an 1832 holding that the laws of Georgia had no force in Cherokee territory, President Andrew Jackson declared famously, "John Marshall has made his decision, now let him enforce it!" During the Civil War, Abraham Lincoln defied its attempt to limit his powers. Franklin Roosevelt, frustrated by a Supreme Court of "older men" that had invalidated much of his New Deal economic legislation, ran into a storm of criticism when he sought to add new justices. He lost the battle but soon won the war when vacancies allowed him to appoint justices more sympathetic to his program.

Sometimes Congress and the states have amended the Constitution to overrule the Court. In 1857, in the Dred Scott case, the Court ruled that Congress had no power to limit slavery. The Civil War and the 13th Amendment overturned this infamous decision. In 1895, the new federal income tax law was ruled unconstitutional—a decision rendered moot by the 16th Amendment in 1913.

The Court has also reversed itself—perhaps most famously in *Brown v. Board of Education* (1954), which unanimously overturned an 1896 decision and held that segregation in public schools deprives children of "the equal protection of the laws guaranteed by the 14th Amendment."

When Congress provided suitable facilities for itself and the President in the new capital of Washington, the Court was forgotten. At the last minute, Congress decided to let it use a room in the Capitol. Until 1819 it met in half a dozen different rooms there. Then it spent four decades in a dingy downstairs chamber. It was not until 1861 that it was given a more dignified home—still inside the Capitol—in what is now called the Old Senate Chamber.

It required the prestige of Chief Justice William Howard Taft, a former president, to persuade Congress, in 1929, that the Supreme Court should have its own home. With the completion of the massive Corinthian structure in 1935, designed by architect Cass Gilbert, the Court finally had a residence reflecting its status as a co-equal branch of the American government.

ARCHITECTURE

The Supreme Court Building, constructed between 1932 and 1935, was designed by Cass Gilbert in the classical Corinthian style in harmony with nearby Congressional buildings.

The architrave above the main west entrance bears the legend "Equal Justice Under Law." A sculpture group represents Liberty enthroned, guarded by Order and Authority.

Above the east entrance is the legend "Justice the Guardian of Liberty." Sculptures of lawgivers Moses, Confucius, and Solon are flanked by groups representing the means of enforcing the law, tempering justice with mercy, carrying on civilization, and settlement of disputes between states.

Inside the building above the Bench are still more symbolic sculpted figures.

MOUNT RUSHMORE
Presidential Giants in the Black Hills

"Volume, great mass, has a greater emotional effect upon the observer than the quality of form. Quality of form affects the mind; volume shocks the nerve or soul centers and is emotional in its effect."—Gutzon Borglum, artist who directed the sculpting of Mount Rushmore

BLACK HILLS, KEYSTONE, SOUTH DAKOTA

In 1923 Doane Robinson, South Dakota's state historian, had the idea of carving a mountain into the likenesses of heroes of the American West. Sculptor Gutzon Borglum was happy to accept Robinson's commission. He insisted, however, that regional heroes were not great enough for his talents and substituted four presidents who had left an indelible impact on the country: George Washington, Thomas Jefferson, Abraham Lincoln, and Theodore Roosevelt. The 6,200-foot Mt. Rushmore was chosen as the site.

The project commenced in 1927. From then until his death in 1941, Borglum, assisted by some 400 local miners, transferred his 1:12 scale model to the mountain, blasting and polishing the rock face whenever weather and funding permitted. They removed some 450,000 tons of granite, leaving behind the 60-foot-high faces of the four presidents.

Mount Rushmore National Memorial, Keystone, South Dakota. The 60-foot granite faces (left to right) are those of George Washington, Thomas Jefferson, Theodore Roosevelt, and Abraham Lincoln.

"A shrine of democracy" is how President Calvin Coolidge described the future monument at the dedication ceremony in August 1927. The Lakota branch of the Sioux nation on its nearby reservations, however, were less happy with the proposed monument.

The 1868 treaty between the Sioux and the United States affirmed that "as long as rivers run and grass grows and trees bear leaves, the Black Hills will forever be the sacred lands of the Lakota Indians." In this case, "forever" lasted until the discovery of gold in 1874.

Sioux chiefs were brought to Washington and urged to sell the Black Hills. But holy ground has no monetary value, and the Sioux politely declined the offer. President Grant, whose Indian policy had generally been one of accommodation, would not take no for an answer. He reneged on the U.S. treaty obligation to keep its citizens out of the Black Hills, leading to the predictable invasion by gold-hungry prospectors.

The result was war—including the annihilation of Custer and his men at the Little Bighorn in June 1876 by Lakota warriors led by Sitting Bull and Crazy Horse. Within months, though, the Lakota were confined to reservations or fled to Canada. Crazy Horse surrendered in May 1877. In September, having left the reservation without authorization, he was captured; when he resisted being placed in a cell he was fatally bayoneted by one of the soldiers.

In 1939, with the presidential heads almost finished, Chief Henry Standing Bear resolved that his people, too, should leave their mark on the area. He persuaded sculptor Korczak Ziolkowski to carve a colossal figure of Crazy Horse at a site 17 miles from Mt. Rushmore. After Ziolkowski's death in 1982, his family continued the project, completing Crazy Horse's head, 87½ feet high, in 1998 before beginning work on his horse.

Crazy Horse's cry resounds through the hills: "The Great Spirit gave us this country as a home.....We do not want your civilization! We would live as our fathers did, and their fathers before them."

But the dream of unbroken history, stretching back to the dawn of time and forward to its end, is common to all peoples. Borglum aimed, in his own words, to place our leaders' faces "as close to heaven as we can...to show posterity what manner of men they were. Then breathe a prayer that these records will endure until the wind and the rain alone shall wear them away."

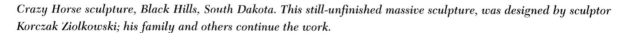

Crazy Horse sculpture, Black Hills, South Dakota. This still-unfinished massive sculpture, was designed by sculptor Korczak Ziolkowski; his family and others continue the work.

THOMAS JEFFERSON MEMORIAL
Author of the Declaration of Dependence

"A wise and frugal government, which shall restrain men from injuring one another, shall leave them otherwise free to regulate their own pursuits of industry and improvement, and shall not take from the mouth of labor the bread it has earned. This is the sum of good government..."—Thomas Jefferson

NATIONAL MALL, WASHINGTON, D.C.

John F. Kennedy, hosting a reception for American Nobel Prize winners, told them that they were the greatest assemblage of talent in the White House since Thomas Jefferson had dined there alone. The epitaph that Jefferson wrote for himself, however, lists only three of his many attainments: "Author of the Declaration of American Independence, of the Statute of Virginia for religious freedom, and Father of the University of Virginia." There is nothing about his work as an architect, scientist, farmer, and inventor, not to mention his long diplomatic and political career: governor of Virginia, ambassador to France, secretary of state, vice president, and, finally, third President of the United States.

But the sum total of these achievements made it inevitable that in 1934, with only one open site remaining for a major monument in the District of Columbia (to complement the Washington Monument, the recently completed Lincoln Memorial, the Capitol, and White House), Congress established a Jefferson Memorial

The Thomas Jefferson Memorial at night, Washington, D.C.

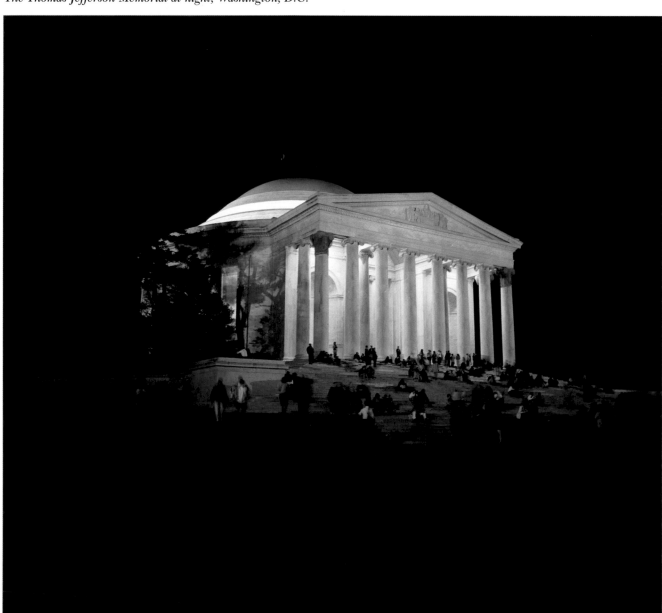

146

Commission. This led directly to the design and construction of the memorial, completed and dedicated in 1943, the 200th anniversary of Jefferson's birth.

Jefferson attained his exalted place in the American pantheon because he was a man of broad education and broad vision, a profound thinker, and a gifted writer. Looking back on his presidency, historians see one immense success—the Louisiana Purchase, which doubled the size of the country and set it on the road to greatness; and one great failure—his attempt, during his second term, to avoid entanglement in the Napoleonic Wars by legally mandated commercial isolationism. Both of these followed directly from Jefferson's basic principles of statecraft and human conduct: expansion by peaceful means, not conquest, and achievement of political goals by diplomacy and economic measures, not war. In fact, of all those commonly accounted "great" presidents (Washington, Jefferson, Jackson, Lincoln, Wilson, the two Roosevelts), only Jefferson was not a military hero or wartime chief executive.

The Memorial, designed by John Russell Pope, borrows from Jefferson's own designs for his home, Monticello, and for the Rotunda at the University of Virginia: a domed structure inspired by the Pantheon in Rome. The major features are a bas-relief of the committee that wrote the Declaration of Independence (Jefferson, John Adams, Benjamin Franklin, Roger Sherman, and Robert Livingston), inscriptions from Jefferson's writing, and, in the center, a bronze statue by Robert Evans. Lincoln, in his memorial, is seated, a father figure; but here Thomas Jefferson stands tall, alert and active, gazing out at the world that so fascinated him.

In many 18th century American towns, Quakers, Catholics, and Jews were barred from holding public office.

While serving in elective office in Virginia, Jefferson called for public schools and religious freedom. He also advocated separation of church and state.

To our modern eyes, Thomas Jefferson is riven by stark contradictions: an ardent champion of liberty who owned slaves, a "strict constructionist" who purchased Louisiana without a shred of Constitutional authorization to do so, a champion of the rights of the common man who lived his entire life in a proudly patrician society. The most talented man in America, he unstintingly promoted the principle of majority rule and worked to overthrow the Federalists' idea that man was in fact created unequal and that the best, not the most, should govern. We may find him enigmatic or wanting. But when we look today at the democratic nation that stretches from sea to shining sea, the land that declares its allegiance to the principle of equal opportunity, it is Jefferson's republic that we behold.

Jefferson believed that the intellect is the key to meaningful human life and to democracy. After the British burned the Capitol in 1814, destroying the Library of Congress's 3,000 books, Jefferson sold Congress his personal library of 6,500 volumes, the largest in the country, to serve as the nucleus of its new collection. After that he turned to his last great task, founding the University of Virginia. That, and the Library of Congress, are the real Jefferson memorials.

LIBRARY OF CONGRESS
Franklin's Inspiration & Jefferson's Gift

WASHINGTON, D.C., AND PUBLIC LENDING LIBRARIES ACROSS AMERICA

The Library of Congress, historian Truslow Adams asserted, is "a symbol of what democracy can accomplish on its own behalf." The country's image of itself fills the shelves, storerooms, drawers, and containers of the library. As Congress prepared to move to its permanent home in the new capital of Washington, it appropriated $5,000 to purchase "such books as may be necessary for the use of Congress." The original collection of 740 volumes and three maps was ordered from London and installed in the new Capitol building in 1801.

The *Boston News Letter* of 1704 was the first of more than 50 newspapers published in the colonies. A few magazines illustrated the wide interests of colonists. The colonies' first printing press was shipped from England to Stephen Daye in Cambridge, Massachusetts, in 1638, and the first public subscription libraries were founded on Benjamin Franklin's model Philadelphia library (1731). The free public lending libraries that followed have allowed people all over America, rich or poor, to have access to great stores of knowledge.

Main hall, the Library of Congress, Washington, D.C. Ainsworth Rand Spofford, Librarian of Congress, championed the 1870 copyright law that mandates that the Library of Congress receive two copies of all works published in the United States.

In many respects, the Library of Congress is the real Jefferson memorial. A national library was thus a sine qua non for the republic. It was no accident that the first law defining its role and functions was passed by the first congressional session of his presidency. After the British burned the Capitol in 1814, destroying the Library's collection of 3,000 books, Jefferson offered to sell his personal library—which, with almost 6,500 items, was the largest in the country—to Congress as the nucleus of the new collection. Washington was in ruins, Congress was meeting in temporary quarters, and the reconstruction bill was going to be immense. Nevertheless, the politicians believed that the country must have a library and appropriated $23,940 for the deal.

In 1851, a clogged flue repeated the British vandalism, causing a fire that destroyed 35,000 of the Library's 55,000 volumes. Congress did not hesitate to appropriate $168,700 to renovate the Library's quarters and replace the lost books. By the end of the Civil War the collection had grown to some 80,000 items. When the Library moved into its new building in 1897, the collection included 840,000 volumes. By 1934, it was the largest library in the world.

Today the Library of Congress adds more than 2 million items annually to holdings that currently include more than 18 million books (two-thirds of them in foreign languages), 2.5 million sound recordings, 12 million photographs, 4.5 million maps, 54 million manuscripts, more than 3 million musical scores, and half a million motion pictures.

FORT WORTH & DALLAS
Cattle Ranchers & Oil Barons

"The Texans are probably the best at the actual cowboy work. They are absolutely fearless riders and understand well the habits of the half-wild cattle, being unequaled in those most trying times when, for instance, the cattle are stampeded by a thunderstorm at night, while in the use of rope they are excelled only by the Mexicans."—Theodore Roosevelt, 1885

FORT WORTH AND DALLAS, TEXAS

In June 1849, Maj. Ripley Arnold of the U.S. Army established a fortified camp in north central Texas, on the bank of the Trinity River; he named it Camp Worth in honor of Gen. William Worth, a hero of the Mexican War. Two months later Arnold switched his base to a site on the bluff overlooking the mouth of the Clear Fork. When the army redeployed to a line of fortifications farther west, in 1853, it abandoned Fort Worth to civilian settlers. By 1856, two stagecoach lines were passing through en route to California.

Stockyards, Fort Worth, Texas.

Oil drilling outside Fort Worth, Texas. Oil is important to the Texas economy.

The Civil War almost killed the settlement; its population fell to 175. After the war, however, the huge cattle surplus in Texas provided the stimulus that ignited the local economy. Fort Worth became "Cow Town," an important stop for the drovers who moved beef on the hoof up the Chisholm Trail to Abilene and other railheads in Kansas. Northern cattle-buyers came and set up shop in town. Stage and rail lines again passed through or made Fort Worth their eastern terminus for routes to Arizona and California.

The closure of the Ogallala Trail to Dodge City in 1885–1886 and the presence of the railroad turned Fort Worth into a major center for the dressed-beef industry. Around the turn of the new century the city fathers offered significant financial incentives that attracted two leading Chicago packinghouses, Swift and Armour, to locate their Texas operation in Fort Worth. The stockyards and large packinghouses spurred the growth of related enterprises like grain elevators, livestock-pharmaceutical companies, and smaller meatpackers.

The Fort Worth livestock market quickly became the largest south of Kansas City. From 1905 to 1955, it consistently ranked third or fourth in the country. Along with the cattle, the city's human population also expanded, growing threefold during the decade after Armour and Swift came to town.

By 1936 Texas was the largest cattle and sheep producer in the country, and Fort Worth accounted for a significant share of this. In May 1937 Fort Worth's total livestock revenues actually exceeded those of Chicago and Kansas City, the traditional leaders. The livestock and meatpacking business expanded even more during World War II, but aircraft manufacturing replaced it as the largest local industry.

Fort Worth also benefited from the development of the North Texas oil field in the early years of the 20th century. Gulf Oil opened a refinery in Fort Worth in 1911; other companies soon followed. Thanks to its location on the Texas and Pacific Railway, Fort Worth became the commercial hub of the new oil exploration and development boom and the home of refineries and pipeline companies. Nearby Dallas soon became home to oil barons.

Changes in transportation, as trucks replaced the railroads, plus the shift from huge stockyards to smaller feedlots, spelled a quick death for Fort Worth's preeminence in livestock. Armour closed its plant in 1962, followed nine years later by Swift. The Fort Worth Stockyards held out for another two decades before the last auction, in December 1992, marked the end of Cow Town. Except for a few tears of nostalgia at the demise of the first source of its prosperity, the bustling city hardly noticed.

CHICAGO

City of the Big Shoulders

"It is hopeless for the occasional visitor to try to keep up with Chicago—she outgrows his prophecies faster than he can make them. She is always a novelty; for she is never the Chicago you saw when you passed through the last time."—Mark Twain, *Life on the Mississippi* (1883)

CHICAGO, ILLINOIS

Poet Carl Sandburg's "City of the Big Shoulders" that we identify with Prohibition, architecture, stockyards, industry, and the blues was, like many American cities, home to thousands of immigrants, Germans, Scandinavians, Irish, Jews, Italians, Poles, Lithuanians, Czechs, Croats, Greeks, and Chinese, as well as African-Americans. With industry came labor troubles, highlighted by the Haymarket Square Riot of 1886 and the great strikes at Pullman in 1894.

The first permanent settlement for Chicago at the mouth of the Chicago River on Lake Michigan dates from about 1779, followed by the establishment of Fort Dearborn in 1803–1804. Its growth began when the harbor on Lake Michigan opened in 1833. The permanent population that year was only about 350, but some 20,000 people passed through en route to settling the distant prairies. Enough westward-bound pioneers dropped out that by March 1837, when the town was rechartered as a city, it had more than 4,000 residents.

Hull House, a settlement house founded by Jane Addams in 1889, served many poor immigrants.

Canals and railroads energized the town. The Illinois and Michigan Canal, linking Lake Michigan with the Mississippi, was completed in April 1848. The railroad arrived six months later. The population tripled within six

Chicago, Illinois, skyline, viewed from Lake Michigan. Chicago, the nation's major Great Lakes shipping port and rail center, is also noted for its meat-packing houses, grain elevators, iron and steel works, and architecture.

In the 1880s, demands for the 8-hour workday became increasingly widespread among laborers. A small group of protesters staged a demonstration and gathered a crowd of about 1,500 people at Haymarket Square. When police tried to disperse the meeting, a bomb exploded and rioting began. Seven policemen and four other people were killed, and more than 100 people were wounded. Eight leaders were tried; four hanged, one committed suicide, and others were later pardoned on the grounds that the trial had been unjust.

years, as new rail lines converged on Chicago, and it replaced New Orleans as the leading port for transshipment of the agricultural and mineral wealth of the Midwest and Great Plains to the East Coast and beyond. Chicago soon became the center of the American grain and livestock trade, embodied in the Chicago Board of Trade (founded 1848) and the Union Stock Yards (opened in 1865).

A major engineering effort in 1855–1860 raised the street level by 12 feet, leaving the city safely above the marsh in which it had been slowly sinking. In 1860, when the first of many national political conventions was held in Chicago and awarded the Republican nomination to the Illinois favorite son, Abraham Lincoln, the population had grown to more than 100,000. Over the next decade the population tripled again.

The Chicago fire of 1871, allegedly ignited by Mrs. O'Leary's cow kicking over a lantern, has acquired a permanent place in American folk history. It blazed for more than 24 hours, destroying 18,000 buildings, including the entire business district, and left 300 Chicagoans dead and 90,000 homeless. Most industry, including the stockyards, was not touched, however, and the crucial rail infrastructure escaped unscathed. Chicago soon arose from the ashes with a business district twice its former size. The burst of modern construction gave the city a push forward in every domain. Manufacturing output doubled between 1870 and 1873.

The Home Insurance Building, completed in 1885, was the first modern skyscraper with a load-bearing metal frame that supports the weight of the walls. All of the great skyward construction of the 20th century relied on this innovation—the most important change in cities since the beginning of urban life, because it removed the constraint of surface area on the concentration of the population. As for Chicago itself, the population, half a million in 1880, doubled within the next decade—making it the second largest city in the country—and doubled again by 1910.

Sewage and industrial offal from packing houses, tanneries, distilleries, and other industries had been dumped into the Chicago River and was polluting Lake Michigan drinking water. Late in the 19th century, the city reversed the flow of the Chicago River, which also reduced diseases, like cholera and typhoid.

Chicago flourished in many ways, famous and infamous, during the 20th century. During Prohibition it wrote another undying chapter in American folk history as the scene of activity of some of the country's most notorious gangsters, including Al Capone and John Dillinger. Much farther from the public eye, the first controlled nuclear chain reaction, initiated by Italian refugee physicist Enrico Fermi and his co-workers (the necessary prelude to the design and construction of nuclear weapons) took place on a squash court beneath the stands of Stagg Field at the University of Chicago in December 1942. After World War II, the concentration of mainly southern-born black musicians in Chicago—notably Willie Dixon and Muddy Waters—created a new sound, which came to be known as the Chicago Blues.

After decades of being overshadowed by New York, Chicago was proud when, in 1973, the 1,450-foot Sears Towers restored it the honor of having the world's tallest skyscraper. (The Sears Tower has since lost that distinction but remains the building with the highest occupied floor [at 1,431 feet] and the most occupied floors [110]). For a city originally built in a swamp, that is indeed a lofty accomplishment.

"Hog Butcher for the World,
Tool Maker, Stacker of Wheat,
Player with Railroads and the Nation's
Freight Handler;
Stormy, husky, brawling,
City of the Big Shoulders."
—from Carl Sandburg's poem "Chicago" (written 1910, published 1916)

CHICAGO ARCHITECTURE

More than any American city, Chicago has inspired architectural innovations. Under the city lies a vast, forgotten system of tunnels, once used for garbage and delivery vehicles. Chicago architects constructed the nation's earliest skyscrapers, and Mayor Richard J. Daley razed poor neighborhoods to create the nation's first public housing (a well-intended mistake). The city's rapid 19th century construction boom was aided by Augustine Taylor's balloon frame, devised in 1833, that made it possible to build a house in a week. Chicago hosted the 1893 Columbian Exposition, which led to the Greek style of public buildings and courthouses constructed across the country. In the 1880s and 1890s, Chicago architects began to abandon the classical style with its masonry construction and to champion the skyscraper with its vertical economy. Elisha Otis's safety elevator, invented in 1857; fire-proofing (after the 1871 fire); and anchoring techniques, like the floating-raft foundation, which distributed and stabilized the load, were prerequisites for tall buildings. The new iron-and-steel frame provided skeletal support; the load-bearing grid lifted the burden of carrying the building from the walls. Since antiquity, exterior masonry walls had grown thicker the higher the building rose. The new steel-frame construction meant that the building's facade could even include walls of glass. Skyscraper architecture and engineering remade cities worldwide.

The 10-story Montauk Building (1882) is considered the first skyscraper; the 9-story Home Insurance Building (1885) the first modern steel-frame skyscraper; and the 16-story Manhattan Building (1890) the first skyscraper totally constructed with a weight-carrying iron-and-steel frame. D. H. Burnham and John W. Root's Monadnock Building (1891) had traditional 6-foot-thick weight-bearing masonary walls at the base, while the 1893 Holabird and Roche addition uses skeletal-frame construction. In reaction to the Columbian Exposition, Louis H. Sullivan and other Chicago School architects broke with classical tradition and began to create "democratic" buildings noted for humane functional design, skillful ornamentation, and vertical thrust. In the 1930s to 1950s, Mies van der Rohe's International Style eschewed decoration, and after the 1980s Postmodernism and Gigantism reinstated ornament and detail. Frank Lloyd Wright's Prairie School houses expressed a horizontal thrust in contrast to the Chicago School skyscrapers of his day. By 2001, Chicago claimed nine of the world's 35 tallest buildings.

Navy Pier (originally Municipal Pier), Chicago, Illinois. Against the powerful interests of land developers and wealthy industrialists, like Marshall Field, Cyrus McCormick, Potter Palmer, and George Pullman, under D. H. Burnham's Chicago Plan of 1901, the entire lakefront of Chicago was reserved for the public's pleasure.

DETROIT
Motor City

"Whether you think you can or whether you think you can't, you're right!"—Henry Ford

GREATER METROPOLITAN DETROIT, MICHIGAN, AND SOUTHEAST MICHIGAN

The French Ville d'Etroit, named for the "strait" (*étroit*), Detroit River, was founded as a fur trading post in 1701. Antoine de la Mothe Cadillac and about 100 Frenchmen began constructing the 12 feet high, 200-square-foot palisades of Fort Ponchartrain on July 24. Two days later, they began to build Sainte Anne, one of the oldest Catholic parish chapels in America. Cadillac invited friendly Chippewa, Ottawa, Huron, and Miami tribes to set up villages nearby to help protect the new trading post. For the most part, the French settlers' relationship with native tribes was amicable.

But Detroit did not remain a French village. British and American colonies fought for control of the Great Lakes and the Old Northwest lands. Detroit's position enabled it to monitor traffic to and from Lake Erie. In 1760, the British renamed Fort Pontchartrain "Fort Detroit," and in the 1763 Treaty of Paris, Britain acquired the Old Northwest and Canada from France. Shortly thereafter, American Indians supported Ottawa Chief Pontiac's war to prevent British settlement. Even after the second Treaty of Paris in 1783, Britain still retained a strong presence and finally abandoned the fort according to the terms of Jay's Treaty in 1794.

The Northwest Ordinance of 1787 dictated that the American government rule the Northwest Territory (what is today Michigan, Illinois, Indiana, Ohio, Wisconsin, and part of Minnesota). It also encouraged free public education, guaranteed religious freedom and trial by jury, and barred slavery. When the American flag was raised in Detroit at noon on July 11, 1796, the population was 2,200. It dropped sharply thereafter as British residents left for Canada. On January 11, 1805, Michigan was formed into a territory.

Like Chicago, Detroit suffered a major fire. On a windy day, June 11, 1805, a fire started in village baker John Henry's barn destroyed all but one of Detroit's 300 buildings. Only an old warehouse and various stone chimneys remained. French farmers on both sides of the river offered homeless Detroiters food, shelter, and sympathy.

Detroit, Michigan, skyline and the Detroit River, viewed from Windsor, Ontario, Canada. © Corbis.

Since America's founding, Detroit is the only American city to be occupied by a foreign power. In the War of 1812, Michigan Territory Governor William Hull turned Detroit over to the British without firing a shot. British ally and Shawnee Chief Tecumseh devised a ruse to capture the city. He instructed his 400 or so warriors to run in loops out of the woods, around the fort, and back into the woods. Hull, who assumed that more than 5,000 warriors threatened the village, was frightened and surrendered to the British. Some historians argue that if Hull had not surrendered, after the crushing British defeat at the Battle of the Thames, Canada would have become part of the United States. The U.S. Army court-martialed Hull and Congress excoriated him. Later the U.S. won back Detroit.

In the increasing Great Lakes traffic of the 19th century, canoes, sailboats, steamers, and tug-barges stopped at Detroit to claim or discharge cargo or passengers. On August 28, 1818, the *Detroit Gazette* reported that the sail-rigged steamer *Walk-in-the-Water* took just 44 hours and 10 minutes from Buffalo to Detroit. After completion of the Erie Canal in 1825, settlers came through Michigan on their way west. Some decided to stay, and Detroit's population tripled in less than five years. By 1837, Detroit Harbor handled as many as 37 steamers a day with hundreds of people arriving from foreign countries and eastern states. Michigan became the 26th state, and Detroit was named the capital. In 1847, however, the capital was moved to Lansing in part because of distrust of the British across the Detroit River in Canada.

Detroit's first stagecoach service arrived in 1822, a substantial waterworks in 1830, and the first railroad in 1831. An East Coast newspaper reported in 1831: "The society of Detroit is kind, hospitable, and excellent. A strong sense of equality and independence prevails in it…" The first road was a muddy trail through the wilderness, following the Old Sauk Indian Trail. By 1835 two stagecoaches a week ran from Detroit to Fort Dearborn (Chicago) on the Chicago Road (today's U.S.–12).

In the mid-1800s lumberjacks cut an estimated 150 billion board-feet of Michigan white pines and other trees, which furnished railroad ties, supplied furniture, and helped build American cities. In Michigan, soldiers widened Indian and fur-trappers' trails into roads and paved them with hardwood timbers. Much of this lumber passed through the port of Detroit.

After the Civil War, the fur trade dwindled. The city turned to manufacturing stoves, steam engines, ships, buggies, and wagons. With the 1855 opening of the Sault Ste. Marie Canal, steamers began hauling rich iron ore and copper from Michigan's upper peninsula on Lake Superior down to Lake Erie foundries and smelting operations. Detroit was noted for smelting copper, making iron, and mining salt from salt beds under the city. Farms grew tobacco and produced cigars, but other foodstuffs were less important to the southeast Michigan economy.

The population grew from 45,619 in 1860 to 205,876 in 1890. A streetcar line with a 3-cent fare was introduced in 1895, and Frederick Law Olmstead transformed Hog Island in the Detroit River into Belle Isle, a 985-acre urban park (one of many today). Detroit was touted as the "most beautiful city in America" and had become the nation's leading producer of well-made horse-drawn carriages, marine gas engines, and machine-made wheel spokes and tires. Michigan's carriage industry in the 1890s had over 125 manufacturers and 7,000 workers. Carriage styles—cabriolet, sedan, and brougham—later became those for autos. Blacksmiths, cabinetmakers, and other skilled workers were valued in carriage factories and makers began to innovate. William C. Durant produced two-wheeled carts, made comfortable with a patented leaf-spring suspension.

With all these resources, engineers and tinkerers put engines to work on the carriages of the day. Ransom Olds experimented in his father's gas-fired boiler shop and shared ideas with his friend Frank G. Clark, who worked in his father's carriage shop. By 1887 Olds and Clark combined the shops and built a gas-fired horseless carriage, tested on Lansing streets. In 1897 they designed the first Oldsmobile, producing four "carriages" that year. In the mid-1890s the first automobiles sputtered on city streets, and racing became fashionable. In 1900 Ransom Olds established the first auto production plant. Detroit was the first American city to erect traffic lights (1915) and issue speeding tickets.

Meantime, in Dearborn around 1896 Henry Ford was testing a self-propelled quadricycle with a buggy chassis mounted on bicycle wheels, powered by an air-cooled, two-cylinder gasoline engine, and steered by a boatlike rudder. The vehicle could go forward but not backward.

By 1904 Detroit, with Michigan's metal-processing and paint plants already in place, was the world's leading auto producer. Ford began production in 1908 of his Model T, which sold for $850. At his Highland Park plant, Ford introduced an assembly line that allowed mass production of an affordable car and revolutionized American industry. His workers built 1,000 cars a day, painting them black because that color dries the fastest. When Ford offered a $5 wage for an 8-hour work day to prevent workers bored by repetitive routine from leaving, he sparked an economic migration to Detroit from the South and Europe. His aim was to sell cars not just to the rich but to auto-plant workers and the broad American populace. Mass production and the low cost per car led to the American love affair with the automobile and the transportation revolution. By 1920 a thoroughly industrialized Detroit ranked as the nation's fourth largest city and had the largest population of people who couldn't speak English.

Robot assembly line, auto manufacturing plant in Sterling Heights, Michigan. © Corbis.

Other automotive pioneers, like John and Horace Dodge, David D. Buick, and William C. Durant of General Motors, emerged. Roy Chapin, who drove an early car from New York to Detroit to prove its reliability, joined E. R. Thomas of Buffalo to form the Thomas-Detroit car. Later with J. L. Hudson, he established Hudson Motor Car Company, which became part of American Motors Corporation. By 1913, Detroit had 43 auto companies and the next year, 69, as well as many parts manufacturers. Only seven remained by 1933, including Ford, General Motors, and Chrysler. Dodge built a test track next to its plant in 1915. Manufacturing plants for all kinds of machinery and consumer goods spread into the suburbs and towns of southeast Michigan.

Workers' unions came to auto plants and led to the 1937 sit-down strike at General Motors in Flint and a walkout at Cadillac, led by Walter Reuther and United Auto Workers. During a sit-in at Chrysler, workers produced a ticker-tape shower.

As roads were laid across America, Michigan innovations led the way. Edward N. Hines was credited with the idea of painting a white center stripe on a paved road in Marquette in 1917, and the first urban expressway was constructed in 1942.

By the 1950s Detroit was noted not only for its manufacturing and mechanical engineers but for gray-iron foundry products, metal stampings, machine tools, wire goods, industrial inorganic chemicals, pharmaceuticals, tires, and paint. A prosperous greater metropolitan Detroit, with one of the highest standards of living in the nation, boasted that 70% were homeowners. Diego Rivera's "Detroit Industry," 27 fresco panels painted in the Detroit Institute of Arts in 1932, summarizes the city's faces, from factory workers to engineers to auto executives.

African-Americans also came to southeast Michigan, first on the Underground Railroad route to Canada, via Windsor, Ontario, and later as part of the Great Migration from the South to the industrialized North. In 1870 Michigan citizens voted to eliminate the word *white* from the state constitution, and blacks cast their first votes. The vital African-American community, with its wealthy professionals and shop owners, grew and enjoyed Detroit's prosperity. But with the Civil Rights Movement came the Detroit riot of 1967 that cost 43 lives, untold injuries, and homelessness. Arsonists caused over $150 million in property damage. The city issued a curfew, and workers, black and white, stayed home to protect their families. After the riots, white flight to the suburbs began. The city's population dropped by one-third from 1970 to 1990 as urban ghettos appeared in once thriving Detroit neighborhoods.

The Michigan economy, dependent on the auto industry and national prosperity, suffers in recessions. "When the nation gets a cold, Michigan gets pneumonia." In the 1970s and 1980s, the oil crisis, massive layoffs, and relocation of industries to the air-conditioned South caused an exodus from the state. Michiganders joked: "Will the last person leaving Michigan please turn out the light?" In the 1990s downtown Detroit was revitalized and the state recovered. The Detroit Grand Prix and the International Auto Show draw people from all over the world. The Motown sound, originating in 1959 with the Funk Brothers, inspired music-industry all-stars.

GREENWICH VILLAGE
Labor Reforms & Gay Rights Movement

NEW YORK, NEW YORK

Greenwich Village, a neighborhood in lower Manhattan, stretches from Houston Street north to 14th Street and from Fourth Avenue and Broadway west to the Hudson River, with Washington Square at its heart. Since the early 20th century, however, Greenwich Village has also been an idea that epitomizes the subversive alternative to the respectability enshrined in Henry James's famous novella and that resonates far beyond the Hudson.

> *"My dear Austin, do you think it is better to be clever than to be good?"*
> *"Good for what? You are good for nothing unless you are clever."*
> —Henry James, *Washington Square* (1881)

Dutch settlers had farms in the area that provided food for the nearby town of New Amsterdam. In the decades after the English replaced the Dutch (1664), the district gained sufficient population to be deemed a village. The designation Grin'wich ("Green Village"; thus "Greenwich Village" is redundant) is first recorded in 1713.

After American independence, the village supplied the kitchen-garden needs of the growing city; farmers' markets lay up and down the Hudson. Successive epidemics of yellow fever and cholera between 1799 and 1822 caused urbanites to flee to the more hygienic suburb. After the last wave, many of the refugees stayed permanently. The population of Greenwich Village quadrupled between 1825 and 1840, as the commercial middle class relocated to the new neighborhood and the affluent settled near Broadway and especially around what is now Washington Square. After New York University was established on the east side of Washington Square, in 1836, the adjuncts of high culture proliferated as well: art clubs, private galleries, learned societies, and the like.

In the closing years of the 19th century, Greenwich Village lost its cachet and property values declined sharply. It became a checkerboard of diverse immigrant nationalities. Soon the low rents attracted impecunious artists and social thinkers, ranging from the merely unconventional to the starkly radical. Factories encroached

Christopher St. in Greenwich Village neighborhood of New York, New York. Site of the Stonewall Inn confrontation in 1969.

In the 19th century on Manhattan's Lower East Side, music halls, vaudeville, burlesque, comedies, melodramas, and farce thrived in the immigrant communities as affordable and often lowbrow entertainment. In the late 19th and early 20th century, these theatres migrated to Union Square, then to Longacre Square, which became known as Times Square. As more theatres began to emerge in what we now know as Broadway, or the Theatre District, American theatre blossomed and audiences grew. Drawing on familiar vaudeville acts—skits or routines with comics, singers, acrobats, and other performers—were the later popular radio shows and television variety shows. Talking motion pictures replaced vaudeville as low-priced mass entertainment.

In 1891, the first Broadway electric marquee was lit on Madison Square at Broadway and Fifth Avenue at West 23rd St., near where the Flatiron Building now stands. Buffoons Weber and Fields began to lampoon Broadway shows at their Musical Hall on 29th St. The Music Hall closed in 1904 as audiences began to neglect burlesque and favor the more respected vaudeville houses and Broadway plays and musicals.

In the late 19th century out-of-town visitors, buyers, convention-goers, and tourists overwhelmed New York. After dark they wanted somewhere to play. The area around Broadway and 42nd Street in Manhattan's Midtown filled the bill with its pricey nightclubs, hotels, and restaurants. They also wanted to see a play, and local entrepreneurs obliged with a surge of concentrated expansion. While theatres could be found all over Manhattan in 1900, commercial pressures and zoning regulations slowly herded them together into a new Theatre District where scores of new theatres were constructed between 1900 and 1925. By 1910 there were 34 playhouses, most of them near Times Square. Ten years later the total had grown to 50; on the eve of the 1929 Crash there were no fewer than 71.

The Great Depression almost destroyed Times Square. Many theatres closed or were converted into movie houses. Then came World War II, which, by flooding the city with servicemen on leave, was good for business.

Broadway is not simply a place but an art form, notably that of the American musical, which emerged from European antecedents to exert global influence after World War II as a medium that was both popular and highbrow. In retrospect, the interwar decades—the era of Cole Porter, George and Ira Gershwin, Rodgers and Hart, Jerome Kern, and Oscar Hammerstein—can be seen as the proving ground for Rodgers and Hammerstein's *Oklahoma!* (1943), considered the first true musical in which every number was fully integrated into the plot. The Broadway musical is an American art form, though it does derive from the operettas, comic operas, and *opéras bouffes* of Europe.

The two decades after the war were the heyday of both Broadway the place and the genre. In the mid-1960s the Broadway Theatre District was on the decline. But even during its troubled years, Broadway's magic persisted and tourists kept coming.

Broadway's many muses, like Stephen Sondheim, Neil Simon, August Wilson, Arthur Miller, Edward Albee, Sam Shepard, David Mamet, Wendy Wasserstein, Lanford Wilson, Twyla Tharp, Julie Taymor, Susan Stroman, Mel Brooks, and Philip Glass, excite theatre-goers. Fresh new plays, musicals, dance productions, musical revues, and other shows, like *Chicago, Fosse, The Producers, Metamorphoses, The Lion King, Contact,* and *Ma Rainey's Black Bottom;* revivals of old classics like *42nd Street* and *Gypsy;* and productions from Britain, Ireland, and Australia, like *The Invention of Love, The Phantom of the Opera, Cats, Les Misérables,* and *Cabaret;* and the works of Harold Pinter, Tom Stoppard, Andrew Lloyd Webber, and Brian Friel, delight even small-minded critics. Each year new talent enters the stage and audiences rediscover why they love theatre. Regional American theatre thrives on the continuing life of productions that first opened on the Great White Way.

NASHVILLE
Grand Ole Opry, Radio & the Music Industry

"Country music is music with a lot of class. It's just ordinary stories told by ordinary people in an extraordinary way."—Dolly Parton

NASHVILLE, TENNESSEE

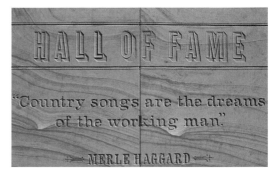

*A*ppalachia is the common name for the southern sector of the mountain range that extends from Canada down to Alabama, and especially for the highlands of West Virginia and the eastern portions of Kentucky and Tennessee. During the 17th century English, Scottish, and Scotch-Irish immigrants settled its steep slopes and narrow valleys. In the early 19th century the rest of the country expanded around them, leaving the relatively inaccessible mountains as the last outpost of a culture that soon vanished elsewhere.

The mountaineers' heritage included the wealth of Anglo-Celtic folksongs, ballads, dance music, and instrumentals. Enriched by African-American sounds and instruments (notably the banjo, which has African ancestry), they evolved a folk music that permeated the rural south and in the 20th century developed into what came to be known as country music and its many offshoots—western, gospel, bluegrass, and others.

ABOVE: *Merle Haggard quotation, Country Music Hall of Fame, Nashville, Tennessee.* BELOW: *Grand Ole Opry House, Nashville, Tennessee. In 1974, the Opry moved to its current home by the Gaylord Opryland Resort and Convention Center.*

Ryman Auditorium, Nashville, Tennessee. Ryman Auditorium, a vision of Capt. Thomas G. Ryman, first opened its doors in 1892. With the coming of the "Grand Ole Opry" show in 1943, Ryman found its identity as the Mother Church of Country Music. The Opry moved to its new location in 1974, and in 1994 the Ryman was restored.

It was radio that first broke the confining cage of the mountains and enabled its music to reach a wider audience. Commercial radio began in 1920, when WWJ in Detroit and KDKA in East Pittsburgh began regular broadcasts. Within four years, more than 2.5 million U.S. homes had a radio set. The growth of the medium was almost exponential.

In 1924, a young Memphis newspaperman-turned-broadcaster named George D. Hay moved to a Chicago station, where he was the announcer for a program of live "mountain music." For most Americans, his program (and imitations soon introduced by radio stations all over the country) was their first exposure to this sound. For southerners who had migrated north and west, it struck a nostalgic chord. And since the broadcasts could be picked up in the mountains, its audience extended there, too. Hay was soon the most popular radio announcer in the country.

When the Nashville-based National Life and Accident Insurance Company started up its own station, WSM, in 1925, it lured Hay back to Tennessee. He persuaded management that National Life's largely working-class policyholders were more attracted to their own music than to the classical symphonic and operatic repertoire. The regular Saturday-night "Barn Dance" broadcasts, initiated at the end of the year, were based on a simple format: amateur and semipro fiddlers, banjo pickers, guitarists, and small ensembles, playing for an hour without interruption. Soon both performers and audiences were pounding on the studio doors.

"Barn Dance" remained an isolated hour in a largely highbrow broadcast schedule. One evening in late 1927, when Hay's slot came up right after a classical music feed from NBC, he told his listeners that "for the past hour we have been listening to music taken largely from Grand Opera, but from now on we will present the 'Grand Ole Opry.'" And that has been its name ever since.

Radio brought music, theatre, and news into American living rooms, making the audience one nation.

The success of the program spurred the WSM engineers to expand their broadcast studio into a recording facility. Other entrepreneurs followed suit, turning Nashville into the center of the country music industry—the self-styled Music City USA.

"A good country song takes a page out of somebody's life and puts it to music."—Conway Twitty

"Country music isn't a guitar, it isn't a banjo, it isn't a melody, it isn't a lyric. It's a feeling."—Waylon Jennings

HOLLYWOOD
American Movies & Dream Makers

HOLLYWOOD AND LOS ANGELES, CALIFORNIA

Movies were not an American invention, but the movie business is thoroughly American. Near Los Angeles, California, and founded in 1911, Hollywood attracted filmmakers from New York and the East Coast because of its cheap labor, bright sunlight, blue skies, and nearby mountains, desert, and ocean. With the Mexican border just 125 miles south, independent filmmakers could escape Motion Picture Patents Company vigilantes. The eight U.S. and two French film companies that made up the Patents Company had restricted film production, exhibition, and distribution to themselves and fiercely attempted to drum out competitors. But Hollywood filmmakers endured and by 1914 the California town outranked New York as a filmmaking capital.

At first, silent movies rarely credited actors and kept their salaries low. As silent films gained popularity, studios created the star system in the 1910s; producers realized that actresses like Florence Lawrence, the Biograph girl, drew audiences to the box office. International silent film stars were Mary Pickford, Lillian Gish, Douglas Fairbanks, and later Charlie Chaplin.

In the 1920s Hollywood attracted talented Europeans and gained a reputation for glamour and immorality. The Hays Production Code, originating in movie studios in 1922 and formally implemented in 1934, demanded self-censorship in response to public indignation at onscreen sexual boldness and stars' off-screen behavior. The years 1930 to 1949 were Hollywood's Golden Age. The studio system flourished and powerful film producers dominated mass-market entertainment. With the rise of television, the McCarthy blacklist, and growing popularity of independent and world cinema in the 1950s, Hollywood's appeal diminished. Actress Marilyn Monroe lamented that Tinseltown was "a place where they pay you $50,000 for a kiss and 50 cents for your soul." In more recent decades, Hollywood has revived and recaptured audiences with both more thoughtful films and blockbuster releases. Americans still love the movies.

The first important big-budget ($110,000) film, D. W. Griffith's innovative silent film Civil War epic, *The Birth of a Nation* (1915), grossed millions at the box office in spite of its Ku Klux Klan perspective on slavery and unforgivable racism. The first talkie, using a vitaphone sound-on-disc system, *The Jazz Singer* (1927) with Al Jolson, drew on minstrel shows and vaudeville. For Walt Disney's feature-length cartoon, *Snow White and the Seven Dwarfs* (1937), 750 animators created over 2 million drawings, copying the movements of live actors who acted out scenes. Ub Iwerks's multiplane camera simulated the effects of tracking and panning of live-action films.

Hollywood sign, Hollywood, California. Built in 1923 as a real estate publicity ploy, the sign is 50 feet tall, stretches 450 feet across, and weighs 450,000 pounds.

For decades, Hollywood supported few roles for women, and those roles were often limited to sweethearts, mothers, and women of questionable reputation. Michael Curtiz's *Mildred Pierce* (1945) with Joan Crawford, Douglas Sirk's *All That Heaven Allows* (1955), which inspired Todd Haynes's *Far from Heaven* (2002), have offered fresh perspectives, as have more recent films. A few actresses, like Bette Davis in *All About Eve* (1950) and Katharine Hepburn in *Pat and Mike* (1952), broke the usual stereotypes in whatever roles they assumed.

Special effects crews, with their engineers, artists, and computer wizards, as well as set designers, are the real engines that shape American movies. In Thomas Edison's *Mary, Queen of Scots* (1895), one of the first American films, a mannequin replaced the actress for the decapitation scene. French pioneer Georges Méliès's film fantasies had influenced earliest special effects. Milk and water created the illusion of a heavy downpour in *Singin' in the Rain* (1952). Crude prehistoric monsters and the giant King Kong of Willis O'Brien's 1933 film are a far cry from the sophisticated realism of Steven Spielberg's dinosaurs in *Jurassic Park* (1993) and synthespians created by Industrial Light & Magic for George Lucas's latest *Star Wars* installment. American films dazzle us with technical brilliance.

Film comfortably ranks as the favorite American art form. Great silent films include Edwin S. Porter's *The Great Train Robbery* (1903) filmed in Edison's New Jersey studios, Erich von Stroheim's epic tale *Greed* (1924), *Sherlock Junior* (1924) with Buster Keaton, and Charlie Chaplin's machine-age comedy *Modern Times* (1936). Important American films do not necessarily follow Hollywood formulas. Filmgoers remember John Ford's western *Stagecoach* (1939), Frank Capra's screwball comedy *It Happened One Night* (1934) and *It's a Wonderful Life* (1946) about the shattered American dream, Victor Fleming's technicolor *The Wizard of Oz* (1939), Orson Welles's Hearst biography *Citizen Kane* (1941) and *The Magnificent Ambersons* (1942) with atmospheric lighting, John Huston's *The Maltese Falcon* (1941) based on Dashiell Hammett's novel with its hard-boiled detective, Howard Hawks's *Gentlemen Prefer Blondes* (1953) with Marilyn Monroe, Alfred Hitchcock's voyeuristic *Rear Window* (1954) and psychological thriller *Vertigo* (1958), Stanley Kubrick's satirical black comedy *Dr. Strangelove* (1963) with Peter Sellers, Martin Scorsese's violent and realistic *Mean Streets* (1973) and *Taxi Driver* (1976), and Spike Lee's *Do the Right Thing* (1989). The Hollywood musical at its best is found in Lloyd Bacon's classic backstage *42nd Street* (1933), with the Busby Berkley dancers; and Mark Sandrich's elegant *Top Hat* (1935) with dancers Fred Astaire and Ginger Rogers and a score by

> ### THE WESTERN
> True to form, Hollywood discovered the ideal Westerner in one of its own residents, Wyatt Earp (1848–1929), who often visited studios and regaled actors and directors with reminiscences of his life as a lawman in Dodge City and the Old West. Stuart Lake interviewed the old man extensively for *Wyatt Earp: Frontier Marshal* (1931), purportedly an accurate biography of a man whom Lake called a legend. Perhaps no other book, except the Bible, has provided Hollywood with so much material.

Irving Berlin; Vincent Minelli's balletic *An American in Paris* (1951) with its George Gershwin score and paintings that come alive; and Stanley Donen and Gene Kelly's *Singin' in the Rain* (1952) about the dawn of the talkie.

Signatures of movie stars Frank Sinatra and Tom Hanks, Grauman's Chinese Theatre, Hollywood, California.

EMPIRE STATE BUILDING
Skyscrapers & the Rise of Vertical Cities

"How about the top of the Empire State Building?"
"Oh, yes. That's perfect. It's the nearest thing to heaven we have in New York."
"Good. On the 102nd floor. And don't forget to take the elevator."
—Cary Grant and Deborah Kerr in *An Affair to Remember* (1957)

NEW YORK, NEW YORK

The skyscraper is a Chicago invention; the first structure to bear this designation, the Montauk Building (1882), reached the dizzying height of ten stories! It was followed three years later by the first modern steel-frame skyscraper—a new form of architecture and engineering that would soon remake the urban scene all over the world.

By the early 20th century, though, New York had the loftiest skyline, featuring the 50-story Metropolitan Life Tower (1909) and the 57-story Woolworth Building (1913). In the late 1920s, local tycoons competed to

The Empire State Building, New York, New York. The building is an emblem of New York and the vertical ascent of modern American cities. An Observatory, opened in 1931, offers panoramic views and has attracted over 100 million visitors.

The Empire State Building, New York, New York. Depending on the occasion, the building's upper part can be lit in various colors.

erect the world's tallest building; it was the Roaring Twenties' equivalent of the Space Race. In 1929, the Bank of Manhattan and Chrysler buildings were under construction, each planning to dwarf the Woolworth Building and hoping to outreach the other. (The Chrysler won by adding a spire that was assembled in secret and mounted only after the bank building was complete.)

John Jakob Raskob of General Motors and a number of associates resolved to build even higher. In September, when they signed the first contract with the architects, the stock market was booming, Prohibition had made it second nature to violate or ignore rules and conventions, and the party had no end in sight.

End it did, of course, the very next month. For those not wiped out, though, the situation offered enticing opportunities, even as the Hoover administration kept promising that prosperity lay just around the corner. The Empire State group could not give up their dream; moreover, it was their patriotic duty to persevere.

The speed with which the work proceeded remains mind-boggling. Only 16 months passed from the start of excavation work in January 1930 until the building was completed. After construction began in mid-March, the steel skeleton rose at the rate of 4½ floors per week. A total of 7 million worker-hours were invested over a period of one year and 45 days (including Sundays and holidays). Even if it was not a miracle, but only the result of some very clever design work by the architects and efficient planning by the contractors, compounded by the plentiful supply of cheap labor in the aftermath of the Wall Street crash (which cut the expected $50 million construction cost in half), the rapid appearance of such a proud edifice was a statement of America's continued vitality, even though millions were out of work.

Almost immediately it became the emblem of New York City and an icon of the national resolve. For those who could not visit the city (and few could, in those years of rampant joblessness), the Empire State Building came to them in 1933, courtesy of King Kong. The giant ape, gripping the radio antenna atop the building in one hand and Fay Wray in the other, remains one of the most enduring images of the American cinema.

For 40 years the Empire State Building held its title as the world's tallest building, until outstretched by the World Trade Center. A few years later Chicago reasserted itself with the 110-story Sears Tower. Somehow the Sears Tower has never been more than a building, though. As for the Twin Towers, they may have replaced the Empire State Building in the 1976 remake of *King Kong*, and they did become a symbol of American patriotism after their destruction. While standing, however, they never attained the mythic proportions of the Empire State Building. How could any earthbound structure, however tall, do so, once men had walked on the moon?

HOOVER DAM

Engineering Marvels

"We had 5,000 men in a 4,000-foot canyon. The problem was to set up the right sequence of jobs so they wouldn't kill each other off."—Frank T. Crowe, Hoover Dam construction superintendent

BOULDER CANYON, COLORADO RIVER, ARIZONA AND NEVADA

Taming the wilderness was one of the great American myths, but it was no myth at all. Clearing forests, building roads, canals, railroads, and other public works: these enterprises shaped America and defined Americans. The size of the country and scope of the task helped meld the individual states into a federal union. Civilizing the largely inhospitable Southwest was one of the greatest challenges of all.

Hoover Dam on the Colorado River in Arizona and Nevada. The dam is the result of a daring engineering feat. America's engineers have tamed nature in ways impossible to imagine in earlier centuries.

Steven Ligouri's High-Scaler Monument, Hoover Dam. Sitting in a chair, hundreds of feet high, the high-scaler set charges to clear loose rock from the face of canyon walls.

In the early 20th century it was recognized that a dam on the Colorado River could facilitate agriculture by regulating the water supply and preventing floods. It could also promote urbanization by providing drinking water and electric power. In 1918, Arthur Davis, the head of the federal Reclamation Service, proposed a gigantic dam in Boulder Canyon on the Arizona-Nevada line. The major stumbling block—the arguments among the seven states of the Colorado basin about the allocation of its water—was resolved in 1922 in a series of meetings chaired by Commerce Secretary Herbert Hoover. In December 1928, by which time Hoover was president-elect, Congress authorized construction of the dam by private contractors working under close government supervision. Although the site of the dam had been shifted downstream to Black Canyon, about 30 miles southeast of Las Vegas, the Boulder designation was kept. In 1930, Hoover's secretary of the interior, awarding unprecedented honor to a sitting president, decreed that the facility be named Hoover Dam. The lame-duck Republican-controlled Congress made this official in early 1931.

Hoover signed the first appropriation bill for construction in the summer of 1930. The $49 million contract was awarded to a consortium of six companies in March 1931.

As with the Erie Canal and the transcontinental railway, the construction site was so remote that roads, railways, and power lines had to be built before work could begin. The Colorado River had to be diverted through tunnels blasted in the canyon walls so that the dam could be constructed in its bed. Like another Depression-era project, the Empire State Building, the dam was finished ahead of schedule and under budget.

Hoover Dam—726 feet high, 1,244 feet long, 660 feet thick at the base and 45 feet at the crest, containing enough concrete to pave a two-lane road from coast to coast, all of it poured in just under two years—was by far the largest dam in the world when it was new. Behind it, Lake Mead stretches 110 miles up the Colorado, covers 247 square miles, and contains enough water to cover Connecticut to a depth of ten feet.

Hoover Dam is sometimes associated with the Depression-fighting public-works projects of the New Deal. It is true that construction took place during the early years of the Depression, that the Roosevelt administration was happy to take the credit, and that it pushed its own dam-building projects—notably the Grand Coulee Dam on the Columbia River and those of the Tennessee Valley Authority—as a means of combating the economic downturn directly. But this New Deal concept of direct action was precisely what Hoover lacked.

His administration trumpeted the dam project as its response to the Depression but saw it chiefly as a confidence-building measure, not as an economic remedy or an example of how government could help solve the crisis. It steadfastly declined to take other government initiatives to stimulate the economy. The rejection, by both the contractor and Hoover's secretary of labor, of the workers' demand for flush toilets and cold drinking water at the arid desert construction site and for compliance with state mining laws cynically exploited the fact that the Depression had made labor cheap and easily replaced. Political rivalries aside, one can understand why the Roosevelt administration dropped the name Hoover Dam. In the longer perspective, though, Hoover did deserve much of the credit for the project, and one can also understand why President Truman concurred when the Republican-controlled 80th Congress restored the Hoover designation in 1947.

> **TAMING THE TENNESSEE RIVER**
>
> Under the New Deal, Franklin Delano Roosevelt established the Tennessee Valley Authority (TVA) in 1933 to revitalize a large pocket of America's poor in Tennessee and adjacent states affected by floods. The TVA harnessed the Tennessee River to provide electric power to crumbling houses, churches, and one-room schoolhouses.
>
> Sixteen dams along the river prevented spring floods, limited soil erosion, supplied cheap electricity, and provided farmers inexpensive fertilizer. These dams benefited people in Tennessee, North Carolina, South Carolina, Georgia, Alabama, Kentucky, and Mississippi.

FRANKLIN DELANO ROOSEVELT MEMORIAL

The Great Depression & the New Deal

"We look forward to a world founded upon four essential human freedoms. The first is freedom of speech and expression—everywhere in the world. The second is freedom of every person to worship God in his own way—everywhere in the world. The third is freedom from want...everywhere in the world. The fourth is freedom from fear...anywhere in the world."—Franklin Delano Roosevelt, January 6, 1941

WASHINGTON, D.C.

Franklin Delano Roosevelt was the first modern president (serving 1933–1945). He toured the country extensively, talking with and listening to the people. He used the new medium, radio, to enter their living rooms and speak candidly to them. Among U.S. presidents, his oratorical skills were matched only by Lincoln; his magnetism, by none. Refusing to surrender to the polio that struck him at age 39, he radiated a smiling optimism that helped the American people overcome the crippling blow of the Depression and then fight and win a bitter war against implacable foes.

"The Breadline" by George Segal, FDR Memorial, Washington, D.C. During the Great Depression, a record number of Americans were homeless and hungry. Proud but humbled by poverty, they reluctantly found assistance in soup kitchens and breadlines.

FDR Memorial, National Mall, Washington, D.C., dedicated in 1997. Franklin Delano Roosevelt was our first modern president.

America has never known a decade as carefree as the Roaring Twenties. The economy was booming; World War I (1914–1918) was a distant memory and no new war was on the horizon; the motorcar gave people an exhilarating mobility. The trickle-down may not have reached rural whites and black Americans, but for almost everyone else, it was a golden age.

In October 1929 the bubble burst. Banks failed, businesses closed, factories shut their gates. National farm income, $16.9 billion in 1919, was only $5.3 billion in 1932. In the automobile industry, the workforce was halved between 1929 and 1933, while wages dropped by two-thirds. By 1933, more than 12 million Americans were unemployed. But the Hoover Administration did little, believing that private initiative and the mantra of "prosperity is just around the corner" would retrieve the situation.

Roosevelt, realizing that words were important but action essential, pledged himself to "a new deal for the American people." During his first 100 days in office he created a raft of new agencies and new approaches to get Americans back to work and make them feel they had already turned the corner. These "alphabet agencies" (the CCC, WPA, TVA, NRA, and others) helped millions of Americans—men and women, artists and writers, farmers, and construction workers—earn a living. The products of their labor, ranging from murals in public buildings to dams that tamed floodwaters and brought electric power to rural America, made the country a better place to live. So did Social Security, enacted in August 1935.

As important as the substance was the public's impression that Roosevelt truly cared about their problems. Actual improvement was excruciatingly slow. The Depression did not really end until World War II turbocharged the economy. Thanks to Roosevelt's New Deal, however, the country had the strength and confidence to fight and win that global struggle. He died knowing that victory was certain, but before the war ended.

In his quiet way, Franklin Roosevelt, although he rarely allowed the public to see him in a wheelchair, may be considered a champion for people with disabilities.

The Roosevelt Memorial combines FDR's inspiring words with images of his years in office: Roosevelt waving from his car during his first inaugural; the despair of men in a breadline and the hope of a family listening to one of his fireside chats; Roosevelt seated with his cape draped over him, his dog Fala at his feet; the funeral procession; and his wife, Eleanor.

The original plan for a statue of Roosevelt standing up triggered fierce protests by advocates for the disabled. Although Roosevelt never stood unaided after coming down with polio, he rarely allowed himself to be seen in a wheelchair. Should the memorial reflect the strength and wholeness he wanted to project in his lifetime? Or should it conform to the ethos of a half-century later and provide inspiration to disabled persons? Ultimately the present won out; four years after the memorial's 1997 dedication, a life-size statue of Roosevelt in a wheelchair was placed at its entrance.

This was not the only triumph of contemporary values over the past. Banished from the memorial was Roosevelt's omnipresent cigarette holder, a major prop in his public appearances: a combination magic wand and swagger stick, the symbol of the smiling good humor and geniality that made Americans feel good about themselves and about their country. Every generation reinterprets the past. Americans have Franklin Roosevelt to thank that they can still do so as proud and free Americans.

HAWAII

Pearl Harbor & Polynesian Paradise

"Yesterday, December 7, 1941—a date which will live in infamy—the United States of America was suddenly and deliberately attacked by naval and air forces of the Empire of Japan....With confidence in our armed forces—with the unbounding determination of our people—we will gain the inevitable triumph—so help us God."—President Franklin D. Roosevelt, Pearl Harbor speech, delivered to Congress, December 8, 1941

PEARL HARBOR, HONOLULU, HAWAII

In *Our Oriental Heritage* (1934), gentleman-scholar Will Durant solemnly predicted war between Japan and the United States, because their economic and geopolitical interests were irreconcilable. The political and military leadership, too, knew what was coming. But many Americans, including prominent citizens and politicians, believed their country was unique, insulated by two broad oceans from the squabbles of the Old World and possessing an abundance of goodwill that could resolve any problems with other countries.

Ultimately, just as it took Lexington and Concord to propel the colonies toward independence, the Alamo to galvanize Texas, and Fort Sumter to unite the North and send the lower border states into the arms of the Confederacy, it took Pearl Harbor to rouse America to confront the dictatorships in Europe and Asia.

The Japanese home islands are poor in natural resources, except for the inhabitants' incredible energy. In pursuit of raw materials and markets for its manufactures, Japan resolved to conquer an empire. In 1895 it defeated China and seized the island of Formosa (Taiwan). Then it defeated Russia in 1905, annexed Korea in 1910, set up a puppet state in Manchuria in 1931, invaded China proper in 1937, and occupied French Indochina in 1941. This led the United States to impose a total ban on sales of oil and other essential materials to Japan. Japan, dependent on American supplies to keep its civilian economy and military machine humming, viewed the oil embargo as an act of war.

In the meantime, America had moved its Pacific fleet from the West Coast to Hawaii and beefed up its forces in the Philippines. In November 1941 Japan demanded that the United States cut off aid to China and lift the oil embargo. The Roosevelt administration rejected the ultimatum but left the door open for further talks, unaware that a powerful armada was already steaming eastward.

Even Admiral Isoroku Yamamoto, the architect of the daring surprise attack, did not believe his country could defeat the United States. He predicted that the coup might give Japan the upper hand for six months to a year, no more. But Japanese leaders hoped this respite would be enough to consolidate their hold on the British and Dutch colonies in southeast Asia, whose ample resources might make it possible to repel the American counterattack.

At dawn on December 7, 1941, 230 miles north of Oahu, six Japanese aircraft carriers and 27 support vessels launched a first wave of 180 planes. At 7:55 A.M. the lead echelon struck military airfields and the 130 ships moored

Hawaii. Lava meets the sea. Courtesy of © the Hawaii Visitors & Convention Bureau.

Pearl Harbor, Hawaii. The Battleship Missouri *Memorial and the USS* Arizona *Memorial represent the beginning and the end of America's involvement in World War II. Courtesy of © the USS* Missouri *Memorial Association.*

in Pearl Harbor. Within minutes, all seven battleships riding at anchor had been hit. The USS *West Virginia* sank first, followed by the *Oklahoma,* which turned turtle, trapping 400 men inside. At 8:10, an armor-piercing bomb ignited the forward ammunition magazine of the USS *Arizona,* triggering an explosion that sank the ship within nine minutes; 1,177 crewmen died with her. By the end of the second wave, just before 10 o'clock, 21 ships had been sunk or damaged. Almost 350 planes had been damaged or destroyed; 2,403 Americans had been killed and 1,178 wounded. The Japanese lost only 29 planes.

But the United States was lucky: the Pacific war would be fought by aircraft carriers, not battleships—and all of the American carriers were at sea that morning. The shore facilities, too, escaped serious harm. The Navy managed to raise and repair all but three ships; only the *Arizona* was so badly damaged that it was left where it sank.

Yamamoto's prescience proved uncanny. For five months after Pearl Harbor the Japanese spread relentlessly through the Pacific and southeast Asia, until their first check in the Battle of the Coral Sea in early May. The next month, the Battle of Midway sent the pride of the Japanese navy to the bottom of the Pacific. After that it was only a matter of time.

HAWAIIAN ISLANDS, PACIFIC PARADISE

In the 5th century, Polynesian people arrived at the volcanic island chain of Hawaii in the north central Pacific Ocean by canoe. By the 13th century, Hawaiian chiefs formed a hereditary caste. In 1778, Captain James Cook claimed the islands, which he renamed the Sandwich Islands, for Britain. In the following decades, the Hawaiian archipelago became a frequent port-of-call for fur and sandalwood traders, whalers, and sealers on routes between America and Asia. Kamehameha I, with the aid of European firearms and a series of wars, united the islands in 1810. Protestant missionaries arrived from New England in 1820, and the chiefs formed a constitutional monarchy. In the mid-1800s, foreign-owned plantations recruited laborers from Asia and began to grow sugarcane.

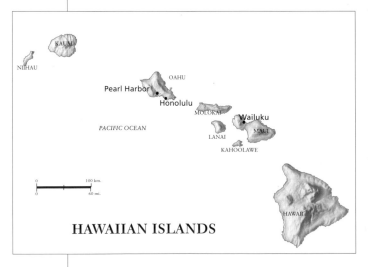

HAWAIIAN ISLANDS

The Hawaiian Islands remained an independent kingdom until January 16, 1894, when U.S. citizens, marines, and sugar planters overthrew Queen Liliuokalani and established a republic. The United States annexed this republic on July 7, 1898 and granted Hawaii territorial status on June 14, 1900. The islands' value lay in their strategic location. On August 21, 1959, Hawaii became the 50th state.

LOS ALAMOS

Developing the Atomic Bomb

"If only I had known, I should have become a watchmaker."—Albert Einstein, *New Statesman*, April 16, 1965, reflecting on his role in developing the atom bomb

LOS ALAMOS, NEW MEXICO

Americans had a proud history of engineers and inventors who, beginning with Benjamin Franklin and Eli Whitney, featured prominently in remaking simple everyday devices as well as the great engines that turn our world. In science, however, the country lagged behind Europe. Only five of the first 93 Nobel laureates in physics, chemistry, and medicine (1901–1930) were Americans. A decade later, however, a critical mass of native-born and refugee scientists, most of them Jews fleeing persecution in Germany, Italy, and Hungary, brought together the theoretical brilliance and engineering virtuosity that produced the atomic bomb.

German scientists discovered nuclear fission in 1938. In the United States, Hungarian-born physicists Leo Szilard, Edward Teller, and Eugene Wigner understood the implications. In August 1939 they got Albert Einstein to sign a letter to President Franklin Roosevelt, alerting him to its significance. In response, Roosevelt increased funding for atomic research.

In the summer of 1941, theoretical calculations indicated that a rare isotope of uranium, U-235, could produce an explosion with the force of thousands of tons of TNT. One day after the official decision to pursue research into atomic weapons, the Japanese attack on Pearl Harbor brought the United States into World War II. Work began on plans to separate U-235 and produce plutonium, another fissionable element, even though no one knew how their output would be used.

In early 1942, theoretical physicist J. Robert Oppenheimer was commissioned to study the feasibility of atomic weapons. By summer's end he had concluded that a fission bomb was possible, though much work would be required.

Entrance to Los Alamos National Laboratory, Los Alamos, New Mexico. Bombs were later tested at Alamogordo, New Mexico.

Henry Moore's statue "Nuclear Energy," at the University of Chicago, near the site where Enrico Fermi and his colleagues achieved the first self-sustaining nuclear reaction on December 2, 1942.

The conditions of wartime secrecy made it impractical to carry out the work at scattered campuses across the country. And because the bomb project was very iffy, it could not compete with other military demands for scarce materials and resources.

All that changed when Brig. Gen. Leslie Groves was named to head the project. Within weeks he gave it a new name, the Manhattan Project; bullied the head of the War Production Board into giving it the highest priority rating; decided that a central facility for designing and building the bomb should be built in a remote location; and named Oppenheimer to head the new laboratory. Oppenheimer suggested Los Alamos, New Mexico, a site he knew from childhood camping expeditions.

Meanwhile, on December 2, 1942, in a former squash court under the west stands of Stagg Field at the University of Chicago, Enrico Fermi and his team achieved the first sustainable nuclear chain reaction, proving that a bomb could work.

While renovation and construction took place at Los Alamos, Oppenheimer recruited staff and appropriated specialized equipment from physics departments all over the country. Experimental work began in April 1943.

Two designs were pursued, one using uranium, the other plutonium. The former was perfectly straightforward, but it was impossible to obtain enough U-235 for multiple bombs. Plutonium could be produced in nuclear reactors, but the implosion technology required for a plutonium bomb was untried and a test was deemed essential. A desert location in central New Mexico, in the aptly named Jornada del Muerto ("Journey of the Dead," or "Death March") desert, was chosen. Oppenheimer named it Trinity after a poem by John Donne.

At 5:29:45 A.M. on July 15, 1945, the bomb—14 pounds of plutonium surrounded by 5,300 pounds of high explosives—exploded with a force equal to nearly 19,000 tons of TNT.

Oppenheimer was reminded of a line from the Hindu scripture the Bhagavad Gita: "I am become Death, the Destroyer of Worlds." Groves's deputy, Gen. Thomas Farrell, observed that "The war is over." Kenneth Bainbridge, the director of the test site, had a more somber reaction: "Now we are all sons of bitches."

On August 6, a uranium bomb designated Little Boy was dropped on Hiroshima, killing 70,000 people instantly. On August 9, Fat Man, a plutonium bomb like that of the Trinity test, was dropped on Nagasaki, killing 40,000 people. Oppenheimer, Farrell, and Bainbridge had all been right. The war with Japan was swiftly concluded. As Sir Winston Churchill observed, when addressing the British House of Commons, August 16, 1945: "The Bomb brought peace, but man alone can keep that peace."

"In some sort of crude sense, which no vulgarity, no humor, no overstatement can quite extinguish, the physicists have known sin; and this is a knowledge which they cannot lose."—J. Robert Oppenheimer

TOMB OF THE UNKNOWNS

American Soldiers Lost in Battle

ARLINGTON NATIONAL CEMETERY, ARLINGTON, VIRGINIA

The tradition of the Unknown Soldier began after World War I when Allied officials found that many bodies of soldiers who died in battle could not be identified. In order to honor their memory, each country chose a symbolic unknown soldier to bury in a monument near its nation's capital. In Arlington National Cemetery in Arlington, Virginia, overlooking the Potomac River and Washington, D.C., stands the Tomb of the Unknowns that symbolizes with solemn dignity those Americans who gave their lives in World War I, World War II, and Korea in defense of America's honor, integrity, and tranquility. An unknown soldier from the Vietnam War was chosen and buried in the tomb, but after his identity was discovered, his family asked that his remains be relocated to his hometown.

The first soldier, from World War I, was buried in a November 11, 1921 ceremony. In 1926 Congress appropriated funds to finish the tomb, designed by architect Lorimer Rich and sculptor Thomas Hudson Jones. The simple American white Yule marble sarcophagus, with Doric pilasters at the corners and along the sides, faces Washington, D.C. The tomb's one-piece capstone was created from one of the largest pieces of marble ever quarried and weighs over 50 tons. Three symbolic figures, Victory flanked by Valor and Peace, are sculpted on one panel. Two panels of the tomb bear three inverted laurel wreaths, a sign of mourning. Inscribed on a fourth panel of the tomb are the words: "Here rests in / honored glory / an American / soldier / known but to God." Sentinels from the 3rd U.S. Infantry Regiment guard the tomb in all seasons and all weather. The sentinel paces 21 steps down the mat before the tomb, pauses 21 seconds, and returns.

ABOVE: *Sgt. Aaron L. Wilson, relief commander from the Honor Guard for the Tomb of the Unknowns in Arlington National Cemetery, Arlington, Virginia, pays his respects.* BELOW: *The Tomb of the Unknowns rests in front of the Memorial Amphitheater, where people gather to honor the war dead, lay wreaths, and watch the changing of the guard. Photos © Jeanette Green.*

AIRPORTS, TRAIN STATIONS,
BUS DEPOTS & GARAGES
The Mobile Society: Planes, Trains, Buses, Trucks & Automobiles

SKIES, RAILS, AND ROADS ACROSS AMERICA

In colonial times, transport was a slow and (literally) painful process over poor roads, most of them originally animal traces and hunters' paths.

Water offered a far better way to travel and transport freight. The years 1770–1840 were the golden age of canals and of flatboats on the Ohio and Mississippi rivers. But travel on those great streams was initially one-way: the current was too strong for unpowered boats to return upstream. That problem was alleviated after Robert Fulton perfected the steamboat in 1807.

But people often wanted to go places that the rivers and canals didn't reach. In 1806 Congress authorized construction of the National Road, running west from Cumberland, Maryland. Between 1811, when construction began, and the mid-1830s, when appropriations dried up, it was extended west to Vandalia, Illinois. The National Road played a major role in opening up the Ohio Valley and Northwest Territory and brought prosperity to dozens of towns along its route. Other highways and turnpikes were built by state and local initiative

Atchison, Topeka & Santa Fe Railway F7A number 347C, painted in the "Warbonnet" attire it wore while pulling the Super Chief. *Courtesy of California State Railroad Museum, Sacramento, California.*

all over the country; the most important were surfaced in stone or macadam to facilitate travel in all kinds of weather.

Came the 1850s and the railroad, with its greater speed and capacity, cut sharply into highway use wherever track was laid. Many towns that had depended on road traffic went into sharp decline, some never to recover, if the railroad bypassed them. Communities offered the railroad companies fabulous inducements to avoid this fate.

After the Civil War, the transcontinental railroad forged east and west into a single country while promoting the development of the Plains states between them. It stimulated industry, mining, and large-scale monoculture. The immense freight-hauling capacity of the railroads made large cities possible but also gave birth to suburbia. Well-to-do businessmen and professionals could move to bedroom communities and commute to work by rail.

Ford Model AA bus. Buses have allowed even people with modest means to visit relatives who have moved away, see the continent, and relocate in distant towns. Courtesy of Henry Ford Museum and Greenfield Village, Dearborn, Michigan.

Between 1865 and 1880, the ton-miles of freight carried by the 13 main railroads increased six-fold, while the total length of track trebled. By the mid-1880s, track mileage in the United States exceeded that of all other countries combined. In the decade 1880–1890, annual passenger-miles rose from 7 billion to 12 billion and ton-miles of freight from 39 billion to 79 billion.

To adhere to their schedules and avoid collisions, the railroads replaced the chaos of local "sun times" (when it was noon in Chicago, it was 11:50 A.M. in St. Louis and 12:18 P.M. in Detroit) with four standard time zones.

After the Civil War the railroads enriched American folklore with famous train robbers like Jesse James and infamous robber barons. The railroads made immense fortunes for some people but also suffered frequent and noisy bankruptcies that left investors penniless. Their rate structures discriminated against farmers and small businessmen. Many Westerners hated them. They symbolized power and progress as well as ruthlessness and greed.

But rail lines could not penetrate everywhere. Large areas were not served by the railroads. The rapid advance in automotive technology in the early 20th century produced a clamor for new interurban roads. Federal subsidies for highway construction were enacted in 1916, and a national highway system was officially launched in the 1920s. Private motorcars, intercity buses, and trucks took a progressively larger bite out of the railroads' dominance.

On land, city mass transit began in the 1830s with the introduction of horse-drawn omnibuses and streetcars. The omnibuses were stagecoaches modified for local service, and the streetcars rode on rails flush with the street, allowing smoother and faster travel. Electric streetcars, also known as trolleys, first used in Richmond, Virginia, in 1889, soon displaced horsecars. By 1902 nearly 94% of street railways in the United States were electrically powered. The first subway was built in Boston as an underground tunnel for streetcars in 1897. Motorized buses began to replace streetcars in the 1930s. The first intercity bus originated in Luling, Texas, when a Packard vehicle was converted to carry passengers between railroad connections. By 1926 over 4,000 small independent bus lines were operating between selected cities.

Air transport began in the 1920s, carrying the mail; passengers merely went along for the ride. The Douglas DC-3, introduced in 1935, was the first craft designed specifically as a passenger plane. After World War II, advances in aviation technology and the construction of the Interstate Highway System, authorized in 1956, left the railroads with few passengers and a reduced share of freight traffic. Eighteen-wheel trucks took over much of the city-to-city shipping business, but made highway drivers miserable.

WALL STREET

Stock Exchange & Financial Capital

"October. This is one of the peculiarly dangerous months to speculate in stocks in. The others are July, January, September, April, November, May, March, June, December, August, and February."—Mark Twain

NEW YORK, NEW YORK

Although it is impossible to specify a single date after which the United States was the most important economy on the globe, there is an epoch by which this was certainly the case—after the Stock Market Crash of October 1929. Unlike previous panics that affected only the United States, this set off a worldwide depression. Wall Street also provides a clear indication of the last date when the United States clearly was not that impor-

New York Stock Exchange, in Manhattan's downtown financial district; New York, New York.

tant: when World War I erupted in Europe, in the summer of 1914, the New York Stock Exchange suspended trading for more than five months.

Wall Street, today a metaphor for the capitalist system, began as the northern defensive rampart of the Dutch town of New Amsterdam. There is poetic justice (if any poetry there be in stock quotations and the chaos of the trading floor) in the emergence of New Amsterdam/New York as the financial capital of the world, given that it was the Dutch who invented stock markets and insurance.

Although the first stock exchange in the infant United States was established in Philadelphia in 1790, New York, building on its Dutch commercial heritage and superior port facilities, soon overtook that Quaker town.

In those days, Wall Street was a dirt path running down to the busy wharves on Manhattan's East River. The first securities traded, on the street overlooking the piers, were bills of lading for the cargoes of ships expected to dock soon. On May 17, 1792, under a buttonwood tree outside 68 Wall Street, 24 brokers formed a cartel, agreeing to trade only among themselves and setting fixed commissions by which all would abide.

Wall Street in downtown Manhattan.

In March 1817 these gentlemen's successors adopted a constitution, named themselves the New York Stock & Exchange Board (shortened to the New York Stock Exchange in 1863), and moved into rented premises at what is now 40 Wall Street. The Exchange moved to a new building at its present site, on Broad and Wall streets, in 1865.

It was then, following the Civil War, with the North awash in war-generated prosperity and the South destitute, that "Wall Street," with its heavy concentration of banks and brokerages, became a byword for concentrated financial power. A business district of Galveston, Texas, one of the country's busiest harbors and a major port for European immigrants, for example, came to be called the "Wall Street of the Southwest"—no doubt with pride and admiration.

The Strand or Avenue B in Galveston, Texas, was known as the Wall Street of the Southwest.

But there was a down side to Wall Street's increasing domination of the American economy. In the Panic of 1873, triggered by the failure of a major investment bank (based in Philadelphia), the bottom fell out of the New York exchange. For the first time, a crashing stock market took the whole country down with it, setting off a depression that still cast its pall over the Centennial celebrations of 1876. Ever since, Americans have alternately cursed Wall Street as the instrument of their ruin and flocked to it as their surest path to riches.

"Buy on the rumor; sell on the news."—Wall Street proverb